DREAMS

Secret Language of the Soul

GEORGE RHATIGAN

AUBURN HOUSE

The author and publisher are not responsible for the reader's individual
dream interpretation; for example, if your dreams seem to indicate health
warnings consult your doctor.

Published in 1996 by
Auburn House,
An imprint of Salmon Publishing Ltd,
Cliffs of Moher, Co. Clare

A catalogue record for this book is available from the British Library.

ISBN 1 897648 81 2

Cover design by Estresso
Set by Siobhán Hutson
Printed by Colour Books, Baldoyle Industrial Estate, Dublin 13

I would like to thank my friend Mary Healion-Shelley for her inspired work of editing. How she could marshal so many weird and wonderful dreams into the ordered pages of this book speaks volumes for her editing skills. Thanks also to Jessie Lendennie without whose help the message of this book could not be received by those who need to hear it.

On their behalf and on my own – many thanks.

My Law – Tieme Ranapiri

The sun may be clouded, yet ever the sun
Will sweep on its course till the Cycle is run.
And when into chaos the system is hurled
Again shall the Builder reshape a new world.

Your path may be clouded, uncertain your goal:
Move on – for your orbit is fixed to your soul.
And though it may lead into darkness of night
The torch of the Builder shall give it new light.

You were. You will be! Know this while you are:
Your spirit has travelled both long and afar.
It came from the Source, to the Source it returns –
The Spark which was lighted eternally burns.

It slept in a jewel. It leapt in a wave.
It roamed in the forest. It rose from the grave.
It took on strange garbs for long eons of years
And now in the soul of yourself It appears.

From body to body your spirit speeds on
It seeks a new form when the old one has gone
And the form that it finds is the fabric you wrought
On the loom of the Mind from the fibre of Thought.
As dew is drawn upwards, in rain to descend
Your thoughts drift away and in Destiny blend.
You cannot escape them, for petty or great,
Or evil or noble, they fashion your Fate.

Somewhere on some planet, sometime and somehow
Your life will reflect your thoughts of your Now.
My Law is unerring, no blood can atone –
The structure you built you will live in – alone.
From cycle to cycle, through time and through space
Your lives with your longings will ever keep pace
And all that you ask for, and all you desire
Must come at your bidding, as flame out of fire.

Once list' to that Voice and all tumult is done –
Your life is the Life of the Infinite One.
In the hurrying race you are conscious of pause
With love for the purpose, and love for the Cause.

You are your own Devil, you are the own God
You fashioned the paths your footsteps have trod.
And no one can save you from Error or Sin
Until you have hark'd to the Spirit within.

Attributed to a Maori

CONTENTS

DREAMS

Secret Language of the Soul

Why do we dream? What, if any, is the purpose of the strange journeys we undertake each time we close our eyes and descend into the arms of Morpheus? Do dreams predict the future? What can we learn from our dreams? The answers to these and other frequently-asked questions can be found among these pages.

Many books, both real and fantasised, have been written on the subject. Mine is based on years of experience as a dream counsellor and therapist. During this time I taught many groups and individuals to interpret their dreams and, through doing so, to improve vital aspects of the dreamer's daily life.

The language of dreams is the oldest form of natural human communication, even predating speech, but it has almost been forgotten as society continues to spiral in the race for ever more sophisticated technology.

Every day, around the world, millions are spent on myriad therapies as troubled individuals search for happiness, improved health or answers to life problems, in spite of unprecedented scientific advances. Yet all the time our dreams, through their symbolic clues and insights, are readily providing the simplest and most accessible information as to how we can heal or avoid ill-health, enhance relationships, and improve the quality of life. By simply paying close attention to these nightly messages, and learning to interpret their symbolism, we can soon develop an understanding of what they tell us. Then all we have to do is to act on it.

Through learning to interpret our dreams it becomes possible to identify and heal the many hindrances all of us inadvertently set up for ourselves.

The purpose of this book is to examine the causes of such stumbling blocks on emotional, physical and spiritual levels.

Each time we sleep and dream the origin of our difficulties – coupled with the solution – is clearly shown even though we may not remember having dreamt at all.

But when we become aware of their value, we will remember those dreams. Learning to interpret them is an immensely rewarding and healing step. Life is not intended to be a pilgrimage or crusade. We have, naturally, certain duties to perform in the course of a day but these are only one aspect of existence. We also have a duty to enjoy living and develop our awareness.

Dreams have many dimensions, as we shall see, but ultimately their purpose is to heal us. The message of dreams, especially where predicting the future is concerned, is always the same; you can change the future if you change yourself. The two basic premises on which this book is based and which are illustrated time and time again are: Everything in the dream is a reflection of the dreamer: All dreams are a form of healing and spiritual guidance.

If we can accept who and what we are, at this very moment, as the sum total of our experiences – not only in this life but also in previous incarnations – we begin to understand many of the seemingly bizarre or complex images witnessed in our dreams. These creations of the mind always contain enlightening messages no matter how nonsensical the dream may appear on the surface.

It is currently accepted that most chronic illnesses stem from psychological origins. Humans are incredibly complex structures and if disharmony exists between body, mind and spirit, it is generally manifested in some kind of illness. Dreams, as a gift from our Higher Self, are designed to help heal such disharmony and increase growth in our spiritual awareness. They also provide a form of therapy which, when we come to understand and interpret it, will help to develop the massive hidden potential within all of us.

In our dreams most of us have experienced unknown people, odd situations, and strange places we have never consciously visited – none of which have any apparent connection with our present reality. How, we ask, could we possibly know these people places and events? Where are they coming from and why? What is their purpose?

Many of the messages in dreams can be easily interpreted once we understand the symbolism in which they are cloaked.

One of their greatest benefits is that dreams can show us why we were born into this present existence and how to make the best of it.

In some cases the (literally) foreign and unfamiliar images may be associated with former lives where we were hurt or caused pain to another. The deed has followed us in order that we may learn and be healed by addressing it.

If the problems we are experiencing in life are connected to a previous incarnation we need to identify and heal them in order to break through negative patterns that may have existed for aeons. This can be simply and easily done through hypnotic regression which is highly effective in breaking old ties. In my years of working in this field, treating people, I never cease to be amazed at the results of such healing.

The issue of sex abuse is one of the greatest psychological

traumas affecting untold numbers of people today and many psychologists and therapists are unearthing cases where patients are recalling incidents of abuse that could not have happened in this life. This is not to say the stories (now known as False Memory Syndrome) are fabricated, which is, sadly, a reaction the survivors sometimes receive. It is not generally understood that these people may be simply recalling and trying to heal a painful incident from a former life. Healing, like hurt, is not confined to a particular time. Later in this book I have documented experiences which clients have had in a former existence and are still negatively influencing their health or relationships in the present. The experience may not even have occurred in the life immediately prior to this one.

Dreams, Meditation, and Hypnosis

An interest in hypnosis and meditation, coupled with an insatiable curiosity as to what life is all about, created my involvement in dream therapy. Inducing the hypnotic state in others alerted me to the similarity between it and the dream state. In both, the subject is in a world of the imagination where logic is temporarily suspended and anything is possible. In such a state it is as easy to relive the past as it is to predict the future. Such questions as: why am I ill? why do I have problems with relationships? why am I unable to achieve my full potential? why was I born? are answered with a wisdom far beyond reach in everyday waking consciousness.

By using hypnotic regression I have brought many people back in time to relive the circumstances of their birth and the descriptions of the experience were remarkably similar. Most told of the pain of birth, the coldness and glaring bright lights of the delivery room, and various difficulties. Many recounted tragic stories of mother's failure to bond in a loving and accepting way with this new arrival. I learned how this initial rejection can colour a child's image of itself and lead to serious problems in later life.

The usual scenario was a feeling of being unwanted and unloved because there were already too many in the family or, most commonly, because a girl arrived when a boy would have been preferred. In the latter case such a female child quickly develops a negative view of her femininity which often leads to adult difficulties in relationships as well as gynaecological problems. In the case of twins one may be hurriedly put aside while the birth of the other is attended. This leaves the first born unbonded and, emotionally, feeling out on a limb for life.

Problems were also caused by the father displaying a state of nervous unreadiness to cope with his new responsibility. The child, sensing this insecurity, develops a similar state within itself which remains throughout life.

Some people bitterly described how their father attended to mother before looking at them. This, to an ultra-sensitive newborn, is taken as rejection. The infant has a limited ability to rationalise and these early experiences of insecurity and rejection form part of his or her self image. Our personality is formed by our interpretation of events on Day One.

My initial reaction to all of this was one of scepticism. I could not believe that a new-born infant is so aware and sensitive. This is where dreams entered the equation because those same people who were reliving, under hypnosis, the circumstances of their birth were also relating their dreams to me. I discovered that practically every dream reflects the impression formed at birth.

Dreams constantly take us back to symbolically re-enact this important event. Descriptions of dreamers crawling through caves, tunnels, narrow gaps, hanging out of ropes, being lifted by the legs and subjected to critical examination by parental-type figures, were remarkably consistent with the accounts under hypnosis of what happened at birth.

Further examination of individual dreams confirmed that these descriptions of experiences at birth, in the womb, and in Spirit prior to coming into the foetus, were indeed true. I found that dreams can indicate the study and preparation each one of us makes in Spirit, how we all accept a life purpose or vocation, and how this life purpose relates to former incarnations in the earth.

This aspect of dreams and hypnosis intrigued me but did not, as yet, explain how quite ordinary people with moderate intelligence could gain access to great depths of wisdom while under hypnosis – a situation which years of conventional psychotherapy could not reveal. To begin to understand I took a closer look at reincarnation. A hypnotised person can often recall and relive, with amazing clarity and emotion, one or more former lives. Using hypnotic regression I reaffirmed that dreams confirmed not only that accounts of past-lives described under hypnosis were true, but also had a relevance to the way the individual lives today. For example, a sufferer of claustrophobia in present time may have died in the cave-in of a mine, in a previous life.

At the end of each account of a former life the subject usually described floating up out of the body, towards a great Light, at the moment of death. Once in the Light the subject met his or her Spirit Guide/Guardian Angel who, with great wisdom and gentleness, helped this soul to evaluate the life that had just ended and to come to terms with its passing.

But, one may ask, what role do dreams play in this? Since the beginning of time myriad races, creeds, and cultures have credited dreams with a spiritual dimension. Many of the ancient philosophers had little doubt they were messages from the gods. The Roman Catholic Church, while not dogmatic on the subject, allows that some dreams are sent by God and throughout the Christian bible we find many of the Old Testament prophets receiving advice, warnings, guidance and prophesy from dreams. Take, for instance, Gideon (Genesis 7.13), Jacob (Genesis 28.12) and Daniel (4.31).

Much of this advice centres on the meaning of life as it relates to the dreamer – in other words, the life purpose, vocation or mission, of the individual. Joseph's dream (Genesis 37.5) about the predominance of his wheat sheaf over that of his brother's tells him of the importance of his particular mission.

Similarly, in the New Testament (Matthew 1.20) we find Joseph, the husband of Mary, learning of his purpose in relation to the child Jesus through a dream.

This tradition of a 'Higher Self' reminding us of a life purpose, during the hours of sleep, continues with St. Patrick. Even when he was guided, by his dreams, out of captivity in 5th century Ireland, those same dreams would not allow him to forget his true spiritual mission. It is written in his own words: 'And there I saw in the night the vision of a man whose name was Victuricus, coming from Ireland with countless letters, and he gave me one of them and I read the opening words of the letter which was the voice of the Irish and as I read the beginning of the letter I thought I heard their voice and thus did they cry out, as with one mouth, 'We ask thee boy, come and walk among us once more,' and I was quite broken in heart and could read no further, so I woke up.'

It was then Patrick realised he had a specific mission and subsequently, as a bishop, brought Christianity to Ireland.

Reading the lives of the saints leaves no doubt as to the respect they had for the power of dreams. Don Bosco who was inspired to undertake his life's work with under-privileged boys after dreaming about scrapping street urchins is another example of this. He too paid attention to what he was told.

But what about the dreams of us ordinary mortals? Do they have anything to say about our life-purpose? The answer is yes, they do, but because they are always presented in symbolic form we need to learn how to interpret and understand this code.

One such symbol is the sun which, in waking life, provides us with energy, life and healing. Anyone who habitually dreams of the sun – or gold, its earthly counterpart – has the gift of spiritual healing. These people have great energy and others feel good just being around them.

Dreams that regularly feature the moon point to the gift of intuition. Such a dreamer enjoys flashes of insight into their own life and that of others – just like the way the moon illuminates waking life and allows us to see in the dark.

Watch too for symbols of everyday objects, such as a television set (clairvoyance – pictures received from a distance), or radio (clairaudience). Nothing in your dreams means the same as in waking life.

At some stage most people dream of flying (astral travel) but if these dreams are persistent and have you flying back and forth with messages, you may well have the gift of mediumship. The onus is then on you to learn how to channel spiritual messages for the benefit of others.

Many have dreamed of being in a claustrophobic area such as a small narrow room, a cave, lift or enclosed passage, and having to emerge though even narrower openings. This is an example of a rebirthing dream which illustrates the circumstances of your birth and will also re-enact the trauma of being born.

Such a dream invariably includes details that, when interpreted, will remind us why we are here and encourage us to 'get on with it'.

In certain aspects all dreams allude to rebirthing. The following example was described by a woman attending one of my dream interpretation courses:

'I found myself, accompanied by a small dog, entering a huge apartment building. I went into a lift and I knew my job was to deliver magazines to people on different levels of the building. I found myself going up in the lift to the seventh floor and then coming down again to the various floors to make deliveries. At one point the lift went through the roof of the building and flew through the air. As this happened I was aware of a Guide advising me not to be afraid.'

Interpretation: This is an obvious rebirthing dream. The huge apartment building represents the mother's body at the time of her pregnancy. The dreamer was aware, while still in the womb (the lift), that it was her mission to deliver spiritual messages (magazines) to people at various levels.

This dream was telling her to raise her consciousness (seventh floor) and learn to travel astrally to higher dimensions (the flying lift) to attain knowledge and information. It was a revelation to this dreamer that she had the ability to channel and was, in fact, born with that purpose.

Rebirthing dreams often take place at a railway station, airport, or bus terminal to illustrate the beginning of our journey through life, the purpose of which may not be as grandiose as that of St. Patrick or Don Bosco but, for us, is just as important. We might be told we are here to learn love, compassion or tolerance. Whatever our vocation, it must not be neglected.

What then of dreams that present us with unfamiliar characters and events of which we have no memory in this life?

Many of us have, at some time, dreamed of visiting old castles inhabited by people in period costume, seen armoured soldiers clanking around cobblestone courtyards, watched monks pray in ancient cathedrals, and perhaps even met the occasional Samurai warrior in the High Street of our dreams. Any clues such as these may well indicate a snippet from some previous incarnation. Former lives, easily accessed through hypnotic regression, are also presented in dreams.

But why do we dream about them and how do those lives affect our present day experience? The answers lie in this Secret Language which promises to enrich our life through the wealth of information contained in it.

THE PURPOSE OF DREAMS

This book is based on two simple ideas:

1. Everything in a dream is a reflection of the dreamer.

2. Dreams are a form of healing and guidance.

Life problems, to which we are all prone, are illustrated in our dreams – along with the answers we personally need.

In order to benefit from this information it is only necessary to learn to decipher the way it is presented to us. The great gift of dream interpretation is that it allows a clear and objective look at ourselves and invites us to change. The choice is ours.

Many good reasons exist for learning to interpret the symbolism in our own dreams and those of others. It is a mistaken belief that this is simply another method of fortune-telling. Although our dreams can certainly warn of impending problems the process is very different from other familiar forms of prophesy associated with crystal balls and tarot cards.

For instance, a fortune-teller might predict an impending ocean voyage, meeting a tall dark stranger, a happy marriage and three children. Or one could receive a dark warning about a business partner having a hand in the till. While this may be interesting, informative and entertaining, it is nothing like the information provided by dreams.

While some dreams do predict the future it is not as a foregone conclusion. Instead we are shown a projection, like a hologram, based on conditions prevailing at that time. We are shown that if we remain on a present course of action then a certain result can be expected to follow. This is the law of Cause and Effect. Foreseeing the future in this way is extremely useful because not alone does it show what will happen and why, but also provides valuable insights into what steps might be taken to avoid the negative consequences of our actions.

Rising upward, or even flying upward, when confronted with a problem in a dream, stimulates the dreamer into a more detached or intellectual approach to a problem. Movement downwards activates the emotions when the dreamer is inclined to be too intellectual. Both motions can be used as a form of healing and will regulate an imbalance in the dreamer.

There are many factors which influence health. Diet, lifestyle, exercise and pollution, are just a few. Dreams touch on all of these, but the greatest emphasis is on the flow of energy or life-force in the body. How we think and feel affects the life-force and, therefore, our health. If, for instance, a reaction slows down digestion and elimination then our blood becomes polluted. Knowledge of this particular energy has formed the basis of traditional Chinese medicine for thousands of years. It flows throughout the body to feed and energise the organs, glands and systems. If there is a shortage of energy, a blockage to the flow, or if that flow is uneven or unbalanced, health problems can be expected. Moreover, if the energy is negatively charged, it becomes poisonous and 'eats' into the body instead of nourishing and healing it. The threat of cancer is an example of negative energy which is bottled up inside and waiting to explode like a time bomb. Our dreams constantly try to defuse a harmful situation and the immune system continues to ward off the challenge of outside agents, such as nicotine, pollution, and radiation. However, it is the way we think and feel that finally pulls the plug on our own defenses. For example, it is not unknown for a grieving person to develop cancer after the recent death of a spouse or having experienced some other personal tragedy. It is how we react to shock and trauma that determines the effect on the life-force.

Every illness which manifests physically would have been indicated years before in dreams. The serious illnesses most commonly addressed in dreams are heart ailments, digestive/elimination problems, stroke and cancer – none of which develop overnight.

It is common knowledge that heart problems, even if hereditary, can be improved by a change of diet or lifestyle.

What is rarely considered is the effect on the heart of the way we think and feel. Yet the dreams of those with heart complaints are as consistent as those of cancer sufferers. Only the pattern is different.

Those with a heart problem tend to be emotionally defensive to the extent they almost literally 'build a wall' around the organ. This 'wall' inhibits the flow of energy into the heart which then weakens. Memory of a painful emotional experience in childhood and a fear of future pain creates a defence mechanism which, in itself, becomes a threat.

While the wall may be psychological the mind has such power that, in time, the thought becomes a reality. Those with heart complaints can also have difficulty in committing themselves in personal relationships.

Mental patterns leading to the development of serious illness were laid down many years before the manifestation of symptoms. The circumstances of our birth and how we reacted to life on that fateful day goes a long way towards deciding what illness will eventually take us off the planet. These prerequisites to disease can and should be detected in our dreams to allow us to benefit from evasive action.

One problem associated with digestion/elimination is clogging of the lymphatic system. Lymph glands are situated in different parts of the body and their purpose is to cleanse and drain the blood stream. It is vital to good health that they do not become clogged. All too often we find, through dreams, that mucous and toxins have built up here. This is very dangerous because it can lead to coronary thrombosis.

Secret worries are also capable of upsetting the balance in health. This is hardly surprising when we stop to consider the connection between mind, body and spirit. If, for instance, we are carrying secret fears of being mugged, burgled, or deciding we cannot cope with life and cannot talk about these concerns to anyone else our dreams deal with them by 'materialising' a particular worry or fear by giving it a shape and size to allow us to 'see' it. This also works well in waking life.

For instance, a popular song during World War I advised everyone to 'pack up your troubles in your old kit bag and smile, smile, smile...'. These words greatly boosted morale and benefited all sorts of people who did not realise why. To anyone with a knowledge of dream interpretation the mechanics are obvious. The listener was invited to imagine his or her troubles were reduced to a manageable shape and size – to fit into a kit bag – so they might be more easily borne. It worked.

Sometimes, in the dream state, our fears take the shape of dark fearsome animals who, if we stand up to them, will back away or quickly become harmless. So too, when calm authoritative friends appear in a dream, we discover our own calmness or authority and can handle our fears more easily.

Helping us to face up to our worries and fears by giving them shape and substance are just some of the many ways in which we receive healing in our dreams.

DREAMS AND SPIRITUALITY

Inevitably, as we delve into the subject of dreams, questions arise about reincarnation, spirituality, psychic powers and the purpose of Spirit Guides. These subjects are frequently referred to in the dream state and we are constantly reminded of their importance to life itself. In order to understand oneself better it is necessary to become aware of their relevance.

Spirit Guides – our Guardian Angels – are highly-evolved beings assigned to each of us with the express purpose of helping us to advance spiritually. They could be described as specialists with expertise in our areas of talent – latent or otherwise. If, for instance, you have healing, counselling, or psychic ability, your Guides, as experts in this field, will prompt you to use those talents to help others and, in the process, to heal and enlighten yourself. When our Guides appear in dreams they demonstrate our particular gift.

The study and preparation for life on Earth which we all made prior to coming into the foetus – our choice of parents and life purpose – was designed with assistance from our Guides.

Perhaps you remember dreams which took you back to a school environment? You are sitting exams and, maybe, have not studied. These common dreams reflect the pre-birth study and preparation time while still in Spirit. Further examination of such dreams will reveal a particular life purpose or vocation.

From the time I first heard of Guides I was determined to learn how to communicate with them. I already knew that altered states of awareness, such as the dream or hypnotic state, allows such access but to help me on a daily basis I needed some other way to suspend the limiting effect of my conscious logical mind.

This I achieved through daily meditation and, in the process, began to build up a relationship with my Guides. When I asked them to interpret dreams their answers helped me to formulate my own system of interpretation which I now share with you.

Because I was dealing with discarnate beings I expected incredibly complicated answers. To my surprise the Guides interpreted dreams in a simple and humourous way, making much use of puns and quotations from popular songs, poems, and literature. Their techniques of interpretation were simplicity itself as this book will demonstrate.

Questions arise as we look further into dreams, especially at their psychic and spiritual dimensions. How does the process of reincarnation begin or end? How do we relate to a deity or Spirit? If we have psychic or supernatural powers how and when did we acquire them?

To understand dreams as a direct link with Creation it is necessary to re-define our understanding of God. We must put aside old concepts, which were originally only meant as symbolic, and, instead, look into our own divinity where we can discover a different awareness of our Creator. The information coming to us from guidance paints a very different picture of creation than that of a patriarchal figure who created the world and its inhabitants in six days.

God has always existed as a creative force but, at some point in history, He became aware of His own existence. He then used his creative power to divide and sub-divide

Himself into other intelligent spirit beings.

The first division – or His first work of creation – was to create the Christ. This spirit took an interest in the developing awareness and well-being of the souls of men who would follow Him as further sub-divisions of God or Spirit. From the moment of beginning His creative work, God ceased to be an individual as we understand the term. He became a collective. Roman Catholic dogma suggests God is a collective of three – The Holy Trinity – but He is, in fact, a collective of all that 'is, was, and ever will be'. The idea of Christ being the son of God properly refers to the creation of the Christ Spirit.

This Spirit came onto Earth from time to time and united with an evolving soul, such as Jesus, who then spoke and acted with great authority.

The 'Second Coming' to which some religions refer will be a visit from the Christ Spirit rather than Jesus and the term 'second coming' is incorrect since Christ has been to the Earth many times from a compassionate interest in the spiritual development of humankind. Next time this Spirit comes it may be to a woman, man, or even to a group, who will then become a powerful force for good on Earth.

The souls which eventually became men were further sub-divisions of God or Spirit. It is important to understand this in order to appreciate and develop the psychic or supernatural power that is present in all of us. These spirits had the power to further sub-divide and each, as part of a Divine Plan, sent a very small part of itself onto the Earth to participate in the work of creation. Being aspects of God they had creative power which was used to set in train the process which would eventually produce plants and animals.

Because the spirits had free will, and were able to reflect their own state of consciousness, they created both positive and negative according to their awareness. Reflections of love became aspects of beauty such as plants and sparkling rivers while less positive states of awareness produced vermin and disease.

Flowers, herbs, and weeds, can be clearly seen to reflect the positive and negative attributes of their spirit creators. Knowledge of them enables us to find cures for various illnesses. Every human weakness is reflected in their creation while they, in turn, provide an antidote to problems arising when similar weakness turns into physical illness. Similarly, animals reflect different aspects of our awareness – a mouse might suggest timidity while a lion indicates courage. In other words we ourselves, as part of the Universal energy, once created the bed on which we now lie. It is important to understand the creative nature of our spirit because we are still creating illness in ourselves by the negative use of energy.

It follows that if using this power negatively produces illness, then positive use of it can heal and cure – not only in ourselves but also in others.

The nature of humankind's present psychic or spiritual gifts is but a pale imitation of our powers when we first came onto Earth. When our spirit body first arrived it was with the best of intentions but, because it became negative and less God-like, it went astray. Distracted from our original positive mission, our ability to harness and use spiritual energy was divided into many negative channels and eventually dissipated.

This negativity – referred to by the early Roman Catholic Church as 'the seven deadly sins' of pride, covetousness, lust, anger, gluttony, envy, and sloth – distracted our soul from its original purpose. Its attention was divided as conflicting thoughts and considerations vied for supremacy. In this way the spirit body lost its power.

The main spirit body – the Higher Self – of which the spirit on earth is only a very small part, was concerned by these contaminating distractions. It wanted to return the soul to that portion of the collective which had not been contaminated by involvement with Earth, or had subsequently been purged, but was held back by the other's negativity.

Through the process of reincarnation part of the spirit returns to Earth, time and time again, to cleanse itself and reform. In each visit it agrees to work on developing a positive or God-like quality such as love, compassion, and tolerance, until such time as it has cleansed itself of negativity.

Each time the offending spirit, by choosing different parents, adapts a different personality and works at developing positive qualities. The Higher Self, in sending these parts of itself onto the Earth, is not unlike a man with an injured hand allowing it to be healed in hospital, one finger at a time. It may, initially, be hard to accept but the greater part of us has a separate and intelligent life outside Earth.

This is what God is – or that part of us which is God. Remember being told as a child that God sees everything we do and knows our every thought? We were not being misled.

The Higher Self is very much aware of our every thought and deed and, indeed, comments on the activities of the day through dreams. This is the means by which we stay in contact with God and are motivated and directed by Him.

However, because we have free will we can choose to obey or not. Disobedience delays our human progress towards greater happiness and development in spiritual awareness.

Through our dreams the Higher Self encourages us to

evolve and develop sufficient awareness in order to escape from this world forever; to be refined or de-contaminated to such an extent as to be free of the earth and its distractions. This process involves returning to Earth, living out a programme of learning and refinement, and working to develop positive or God-like qualities.

Dreams are a form of communication between God, our Higher Self which is all-wise and all-knowing, and the aspect we call our personality which is trapped on the earth by its own limited awareness. Our dreams help us to develop positive qualities through using our gifts and and recognising our divinity. We utilised these miraculous powers when we first came to Earth, even participated in its creation, so why can we not use them now? Only because we are not in a state of harmony, divided as we are, against ourselves. However, through an enjoyably centering practise – like meditation – and becoming more in tune with the main spirit body or Higher Self, we can reclaim some of these powers and use them for healing and helping each other.

From time to time, through the ages, healers and magicians distinguished themselves and seemed to possess miraculous powers. They were thought to be either gods or devils and many were burnt to death as witches – all because they came close to recapturing some of these ancient abilities which are ours by right.

Jesus was one such magician. He used his power to heal the sick and tried to tell his followers that others could do even better:

> *I tell you most solemnly, whoever believes in me will perform the same works as I do myself, he will perform even greater works.*
>
> (John 14:12)

Jesus shared this healing philosophy with his disciples. His secret was to heal by love. 'Love God, love yourself, and love your neighbour,' was His message. He healed with faith (oneness of mind) and love (the positive, God-like, quality).

In order to heal or produce a positive effect we must send out a positive message. This cannot be done effectively if one is full of anger or resentment. The second and equally essential part of re-impowerment is concentration or being 'at one' with your intention to heal or to use whatever power or gift you have. As distinct from being 'at one', most of us are in two minds about everything we do, forever balancing other considerations and allowing distractions to get in our way. Faith in ourself drives out fear and leads to oneness of mind.

The present phenomenal interest in meditation as a means of developing spiritual gifts is due to the concentration of the mind that meditation or hypnosis produces. It enables a person to be at one with him or herself – if only for a limited period of time – while tapping into this power source. The message of dreams concerning our spiritual powers is: Do it with love. Be at one with your power.

When we come to the end of this present incarnation we will all experience death. While this is regarded as a cause for grief among those who love us on the earth plane, the event is celebrated in the spirit world where the new arrival is welcomed with great rejoicing. Similarly a birth on earth is a bereavement in spirit for a lost friend – albeit temporarily.

A popular old wives tale in Ireland holds that to dream of a death indicates a birth and vice versa. Although I have never known this to be true when applied to the physical world, I regard death and birth in dreams as change and renewal.

When our presence is required in the next world we will be invited to 'pass over' in a pleasant way through our dreams. Free will is always present of course so we can, by declining the invitation, remain on earth for many more years.

Examples

An elderly woman asked me to interpret the following dream: She was back in the rural area where she lived as a child. In her dream she was at the end of a little lane and the whole area was surrounded with the most beautiful flowers of every colour.

Interpretation: Her dream asked this old woman to accept the inevitability of her death (end of the lane) and to accept with love (the flowers) congratulations on a job well done.

In another dream a man was in a boat and had to pass through a series of channels. At the entrance to each stood a man who, like a lock keeper, exacted a toll from all who passed. He gave up his cargo to one such keeper and was asked to pass to the next channel. He gave his clothes to the next man and passed naked into the following channel. Finally, all he had left was his watch which he handed to the last man.

Interpretation: The meaning was obvious and indicated the need for this dreamer to let go of material possessions as he gradually passed from earthly life. Eventually all he has left was a little time (the watch) which he willingly gave up thereby ensuring a peaceful passing. This dreamer died six weeks later.

In contrast to the painful process of birth, death is a pleasant release, as those who have had a near-death experience will testify. One such brush with death occurred to a friend when she had a near-fatal heart attack. She found herself in a beautiful landscape where she experienced a wonderful sense of peace. 'It was,' she said, 'like the inside of a buttercup'. So pleasant was her experience that when she was resuscitated and her heart was beating strongly again, she was annoyed to find herself back on earth.

That week she had the following dream: She was in Dublin on O'Connell Bridge (the transitional state between life and death) and a policeman was directing traffic. (Like the lock-keeper in the previous dream this figure of authority represents the Guardian Spirit on the Threshold.)

This policeman held up one hand to prevent two horses from leaving a building (separation of the animal or physical body at death) and with the other hand prevented pedestrians from passing over the bridge. She was among these pedestrians and tried to force her way against his signal.

Interpretation: She was not meant to die yet.

A touch of the ecstasy that is the Spirit Plane replaces all fear of death with a feeling of tranquillity and a deep desire to return when the time comes. People who have had this experience know there is nothing to fear. There will be no harsh Judgement, no Heaven or Hell in the generally accepted sense but, instead, a more intense form of what we experience every night in the deeper levels of sleep. In these levels, when we are not dreaming, we telepathically leave our bodies and communicate with Guides, departed relatives and friends. This area of communication is known as the Astral Plane.

Each night our Guide comments on our thoughts and

activities of the day and to what extent we remained faithful to our life plan and our Higher Self, with a cleverly devised dream, gives us healing and guidance in this regard. We are shown what steps to take in order to further these aims. In addition we are expected to work in this Astral plane in the service of others. In a similar way others will help us and, all the while, the work is carried out telepathically.

Death is similar in that, once again, we function telepathically without a body. Naturally, in both states, free will is paramount and we can choose not to work – in which case neither will we ourselves develop. On the Astral, as with the Spirit plane, there are 'many mansions' or different levels of existence and experience. The nature of the place or state we go to when we sleep, or die, is determined by our state of mind.

For instance, if we go to sleep in a bad humour we find ourself on a similar level in the Astral where we will meet entities of like mind or disposition. For this reason humankind has long been encouraged to live in a 'state of Grace' in preparation for the end of physical life.

RULES FOR DREAM INTERPRETATION

It is not difficult to interpret a dream. Think of it as a short play divided into ten basic segments. These are Characters and Roles (as in Adults, Children and Animals) Location, Objects, Colours, Activities, Emotions and, oddly, Puns. We begin by considering each of these individually before putting them back together in the order we dreamt them.

The same symbols appear repeatedly in different people's dreams and carry, in general terms, the same meaning. A simple set of rules may be applied to make sense of such symbols although these are not like the exacting rules of science but rather are intended to be viewed as guidelines. As with every other aspect of nature it is our intuition, knowledge, and experience that will carry us the rest of the way.

Rule One:
Everything is Me

Dreams, being creations of the mind, reflect such aspects of the personality as ideas, ideals, emotions, hopes, fears, health and sexuality. They recreate our functioning which has four basic outlets of expression, (A) Physical (B) Emotional (C) Mental (D) Spiritual.

A. Solid symbols, such as a house, car, or the earth, represent the body. For example, if the structure of the house in your dream is shown as in need of repair, it indicates poor physical health in the present or future.

B. Fiery symbols, as in fire, electricity, bombs or gunfire, symbolise the emotions. If emotion – or lack of it – is a problem then look for reference to these fiery symbols. Take note of the effect they have on the solid structure in your dreams such as lightening striking a house or fire consuming a hospital. Such dreams contain health warnings.

Sometimes, the sources of heat, or emotion, are conspicuous by their absence as, for instance, a dream about a fireplace with an unlit fire in the hearth – a pun for heart. This indicates the repression of normal emotional expression which, in waking life, can lead to physical problems with the heart. The same dream might draw your attention to a crack in the chimney wall indicating problems with the circulatory system in present or future time. The heart needs the stimulus of emotion to stay healthy.

C. Airy or ethereal symbols, such as the wind, atmosphere, weather, the interior of a room or building – literally the space between the four walls – indicate your state of mind. For example, darkness to the front of a house or building can indicate a depressing or pessimistic view of life or the world. A 'heavy' leaden sky carries a similar meaning, while a dingy, dirty room with filthy furniture and old rags scattered around indicates an angry state of mind. The way we decorate or desecrate our rooms in waking life is a reflection of the way we think and the same is true in our dreams.

D. Water symbols such as rivers, lakes, canals, the sea, household water, rain and even bodily fluid, reflect the dreamer's philosophy of life, his spiritual expression – as in music, art, religion, psychic awareness – and the bloodstream. For example, if a dream features a man-made canal which is geometrically structured and artificial, then spiritual expression is limited rather than natural and free-flowing. This can indicate influence from a rigid form of structured religion. A contained source of water, like a lake or pond, indicates the dreamer has no outlet for spiritual expression, especially if the water is stagnant. Material considerations – land surrounding the water – are inhibiting spiritual flow.

If the waterway is dirty and polluted – a river, stream or canal with sewage, plastic bags, rubbish or other waste matter floating or being dumped into it – then the dream may be indicating the state of your blood stream. This usually means that toxic waste from the colon is entering and polluting the circulatory system.

A polluted waterway can also indicate a sense of guilt and a need to feel 'clean'. This usually comes from former life (religious) influences.

Rule Two:
Cause and Effect

Everything in a dream is linked to everything else to show Cause and Effect. In applying this rule we find that apparently unconnected emotions, characters, events and objects are symbolically linked, however illogically, to illustrate this.

Look for a symbol to indicate the Cause of the dreamer's problem and another symbol to show the Effect. Future indications are often shown in this way because if the dreamer is not experiencing the effect at present then he or she will in future. The cause of the problem, usually in the past, will be established at an early stage – perhaps during the first two sentences of the dreamer's account. It is often connected with his or her emotional response to parents and is often indicated by a character or location described in a negative way – for example, 'the kitchen was dirty when the woman came in' – digestive problems linked to the dreamer's mother.

This rule may also be applied to show why the dreamer limits his or her gifts, talents or powers, is, depressed, or cannot get on with a spouse, boss, partner, why his or her career is not getting off the ground, or why other life troubles of this kind are occurring.

Rule Three:
I am Responsible

The dreamer is always, without argument, personally responsible for what is happening, has, can, or will happen in a dream.

In this state we find all kinds of apparent accidents, blockages to progress, and other impediments to movement. On the surface these may seem to be out of our control but in applying Rule Three we assume responsibility for our progress.

Take a dream that shows delays at an airport. This clearly illustrates a reluctance to get some new new project off the ground. Road blocks or obstructions in the dreamer's path mean a reluctance to clear obstacles to progress.

Rule Four:

*What I try to avoid in a dream
is what I need most in waking life.*

This rule is similar to the previous one in that both refer to the way we can control or 'spoil' our dreams. Even subconsciously we have the ability to change the dream and the characters appearing in it if we do not want to accept what it is telling us.

A dream is not simply a message coupled with healing but is also our response or reply to this. Our Higher Self decides we need healing and guidance in a particular area of life and a dream is dispatched expressly for this purpose. In it we are asked to accept and develop a positive quality in accordance with our agreed life purpose. This quality might, for instance, be compassion because in a former life we had a tendency to judge ourselves or others too harshly. Such a pattern of self-criticism re-appears in this life to threaten our emotional and physical well-being, and must be eradicated if we are not to suffer the consequences. Such a situation can be shown in a dream like the following:

A kindly judge (Guide) sits on the bench as friendly advocates (Healing Agents) plead our case. (This shows we are asked to soften a rigid judgmental attitude and show compassion to ourselves.) Initially all is well but then things begin to go awry. The dreamer cannot hear the judge. Defence counsel now appears as a foreigner speaking an incomprehensible language. The dreamer is found guilty and sentenced to death. When Rule Three is applied to the dream it becomes apparent the dreamer brought it on himself by his negative expectations.

Rule Four asks us to look for what we have been avoiding. This will always be shown as a positive quality or the means to acquire it.

To accept and develop this the dreamer may be asked to eliminate its negative counterpart as in the previous sample where harsh judgement precludes compassion.

Another person may be asked to develop humility in a dream that emphasises arrogance or to show forgiveness instead of resentment. Such dreams will often show the consequences of negativity (Rule Two) in terms of emotional upset or ill health.

Here are some examples of how these rules work:

A young man dreamt he was walking with his girlfriend along a narrow blind alley. Some distance ahead they could see a number of women who were screaming hysterically as they pointed to an object on the ground. As the couple got closer they saw the object was a human head. It was hairless and was opening and closing its mouth in a vain attempt to speak. Then the dreamer was horrified to recognise it as his own head.
(Key Words: Narrow, Blind, Hairless, Vain.)

Interpretation: This young man was losing his head over his girlfriend. The blind alley suggested he could not get a clear overall view of the relationship. The hysterical reaction of the women suggested he was veering towards a great deal of emotional upset. Women in dreams can represent the emotions or emotional response to one or more particular females in waking life. In this case it was to the dreamer's girlfriend.

This dream also makes a prediction that is illustrated as Cause and Effect. The Cause is his 'blind alley' or blinkered response to his partner and the Effect – futuristic as he had not experienced it up to then – is the hysteria. Passage of time is indicated by the movement along the alley.

The head, being without hair, is further indication of his inability or unwillingness to think. Hair, like thoughts and ideas, grows out of the head. The state or colour of hair in a dream indicates the dreamer's state of mind.

Very shortly after having this dream the young man's girlfriend ditched him. This created a terrible state of emotional upheaval for him.

A young housewife consulted me regarding her weight problem. In spite of numerous attempts at slimming she found she could not retain weight loss for any length of time. The night before we met she dreamt she was in a public house. She sat opposite another woman in a blonde wig whom she described as 'grotesque'. This person, had a thin bony face, limbs and shoulders, 'like a refugee from a famine area' except that on her chest and lower body were heavy layers of fat. The strange creature explained she was on a diet. The dreamer reacted to her in alarm.

(Key Words : Thin, Bony, Grotesque.)

Interpretation: The location of this dream, a public house, tells something of the dreamer's state of consciousness in relation to social contact. The frailty of her companion (herself) indicates feeling emotionally vulnerable when dealing with people in a social context, even though the blonde wig shows she, the dreamer, maintains an outward appearance of positivity. Caricatures like this often carry the cause and effect in their composition i.e. sensitivity (the bony part) and insulation (the fatty part). She uses layers of fat as a buffer against being hurt by other people. Because, at some stage in her youth, the dreamer's mind had formed a link between confidence and bodily weight no diet would work for her. As soon as she began to lose weight, she would feel insecure.

This is typical of the dreams of women who are grappling with weight problems. Many sensitive women who feel vulnerable in their body react by insulating it with fat, regardless of how much or how little they eat in an effort to allay their fears of coping with life as a female.

Such fears manifest in dreams in a variety of ways. It may be in the appearance of emaciated females – sometimes naked, sick, dying or in a cold bare room. Alternatively overdressed or overweight women may appear – even taking a bath or shower while fully clothed. The meaning is still the same – protecting herself, subconsciously, with excess body fat or too many clothes.

Another dream came from a 35-year-old unmarried woman who was suffering from a stammer and described herself as being reserved and undemonstrative.

In the dream she was back in a part of a city where she lived as a child. The place was deserted and she was standing alone in the street. All the shops were closed with great steel shutters covering the (front) windows. In the distance she could hear sounds of an approaching demonstration. As the sound came closer she became aware that men and women were involved in the march and she became greatly alarmed.

(Key Words : Closed, Shuttered, Steel, Alarmed(Effect).

Interpretation: Being taken back to a childhood scene is a familiar device used in dreams. This indicates the problem which the dream is addressing has its origins in the past. The dreamer saying 'I was alone' indicates fear and a sense of isolation. But, in this case, fear of what? The demonstrators provide a clue in that the are demonstrating which suggests fear of being demonstrative. Since both men and women are involved in this it indicates the dreamer's fears are linked to emotional (female) and intellectual (male) expression. Since the demonstrators were exercising freedom of speech the dream emphasised what this dreamer lacked – hence the stammer.

The following chapters explain further aspects of dreams in greater detail.

APPLYING THE RULES FOR SUCCESS

The new approach to life that our dreams advise us to develop may be completely alien to our usual mode of behaviour. It may be so strange to us that when our Guides or Healing Agents appear it is as obvious foreigners or even as beings from another planet. As a result we may well resist the teaching by trying to change the dream, to 'spoil' it by running away, or wake up before it ends.

Sometimes our dreams ask us to participate in activities which we can also experience in waking life to help our positive qualities grow. Sex, affection or intimacy can help us to appreciate love. Child-bearing, nursing, or fostering children, encourages maturity or greater responsibility. Teaching, writing, or expressing oneself through other forms of art, may bring about greater objectivity or a deeper understanding of life.

In order to develop generosity, or learn to share ourself emotionally, a Guide may appear and demonstrate one's natural healing or psychic ability if he or she is expected to use these gifts in the service of others. The dreamer may initially respond and participate with enthusiasm but then find this changing to a situation where he or she takes instead of gives – or reacts to others as if they were thieves who would steal everything. This is an instance of the dreamer's fears intervening and 'spoiling' the dream. Anyone who believes psychic work to be evil might find the Guide changing into something like a 'black devil'. This is how we project our fears onto characters in a dream who are simply trying to lead us by example or to heal us with positivity.

If, in a dream, you refuse to marry or become intimate with an older partner or, if you chop down a mature tree in your garden, it indicates you are trying to avoid emotional maturity.

Running away from an animal because it is dirty, ugly or threatening to smother means the dreamer is uncomfortable with sexuality, intimacy, affection, or with the instinctive side of life.

The positive quality such a dreamer came into this life to develop may be an openness to accept new ideas. If so, this could be presented as young men or boys (male aspects: ideas) appearing in the dreamer's house or knocking on the door. The reaction may be fear and panic. Dangerous burglars have broken in. The dreamer runs away or angrily ejects them from the building.

In our efforts to avoid the positive quality we attempt to limit or repress the outlet of expression that could lead to its development much as we do in waking life. To work out how this appears in dreams it helps to write them out and to note the emotions experienced as they unfolded.

Once this is done it is important to scan the dreams and watch out for the following, or any similar key words or phrases of limitation, avoidance or containment: Arid, avoid, blind, blocked, box, broken, cage, chaos, closed, cold, control, Cork city (pun), dark, dead, deaf, deformed, deny, dilapidate, delay, destroy,drug, eject, fight, frozen, grey, hard, hit, ignore, injure, isolate, kill, lame, lock, missing, mutate, narrow, neglect, obstruct, 'on the fence' (pun for uncommitted), pack, pollute, poor, prison, rat, rectangle, refuse, regimented, resist, reject, scatter, shelter, sick, sneer, square, stain, starve, stifle, stop, strangle,tie, trap, unbalance, uneven, unlit, unpaid, unready, wall, waste, weak, wither, worm.

To what are such words applied? What, for instance, was arid, starved, or withered? Was it in a box or square? This symbolises an aspect of the dreamer's functioning that he or she is limiting or repressing in waking life. For example, in a dream that says, 'The dead woman was lying on the cold hard slab', the Key Words are 'dead', 'lay', 'cold', 'hard' all of which indicate the dreamer has limited emotional or female expression (Rule Three). The previous list, coupled with the following, represents 'Effect' in a dream (Rule Two) although further effect may be indicated later. 'Cause' is established by (a) negative emotions evoked by the dream and (b) any Key Words which would imply such feelings: Afraid, alone, angry, anxious, beneath me, black/white, dangerous, despise, devil, doubt, evil, hate, intrude, jealous, selfish, terrified, trap, etc. This exercise helps to match Cause with Effect.

An obvious example would be dreaming of a nun in a black and white habit who appears in a bedroom that contains a press (cupboard), or closet. The 'habit' (pun) of negative religious conditioning (fear) leads to repression – the 'press' – or closeting of the dreamer's sexuality (Cause and Effect).

A simple method of working out what the dream is telling us on a very basic level is to write it out in detail and then make two headings reading 'I AM' and 'I NEED'. Under the first heading list all the words of limitation from your written dream description. By applying these to yourself in relation to the subject matter as indicated by the location it will help you to see what is holding you back. Then, under the heading of 'I NEED' list all the positive words or phrases – those which indicate positive qualities.

For example: 'The restaurant was very packed and the

service (movement of food) was extremely slow.'

The subject matter is the dreamer's digestion (restaurant) and the Key Words refer to sluggish digestion and elimination. 'Then a waiter came and quickly removed the dirty plates.'

When listed under 'I NEED' these Key words suggest the dreamer needs to develop patience, a positive quality, i.e. to learn how to wait and eliminate waste quickly from the body.

Colours may also be listed under 'I AM' and 'I NEED and the words 'I AM' must also be applied to the solid objects in the dream as in Rule One.

Our Masculine/Feminine Self

Human functioning is divided into two basic categories, masculine and feminine. All of us, regardless of gender, have or are meant to have, the appropriate amount of male and female energy and expression. This ensures our glands produce the correct amount of male and female hormones. The male side helps us to be creative, logical, confident, individualistic, responsible, decisive and so on, when this aspect is healthily active. The female side, on the other hand, is passive, caring, nurturing, sensitive and intuitive.

If the positive quality we were born to develop fits into the masculine category – e.g. courage or assertiveness – and we are limiting this quality our dreams will, on a regular basis, feature men sitting down ('sitting down on the job') men lying down ('not standing up for ourselves') or those men will be depicted as thin, weak or, perhaps, disabled.

This aspect, which also governs the human sex drive, is illustrated by phallic symbols such as obelisks, poles, guns, rods, etc. Damage to, or rejection of, any such symbol indicates loss of potency – not just in the sexual sense but in general assertiveness, ambition and other aspects of male expression.

More commonly it is the feminine aspect that is stunted. This may be indicated in dreams by females falling down, in a wheelchair, emaciated, drunk (blotting out emotion and/or sensitivity) or in other negative situations.

The feminine side of our nature influences the emotional and sensual element of our sexuality. This is indicated in dreams as containers, cavities, skirts, dresses, canopies or other female symbols. Indications of difficulty with this aspect of ourselves, or a tendency to limit its positive qualities, will be shown in our dreams as damage, reluctance, limitation, dark negative colours or unpleasant shades associated with any of the above symbols. An example of this is a dream of a woman wearing a black dress or washing in a dirty bath – the 'unclean vessel'.

When we write down our dreams and we read through them, applying the rules of interpretation, it becomes clear how we are limited and disempowered by negativity.

Dreams focus on this by drawing attention to; selfishness, extremism, resentment, cynicism, materialism, arrogance, intolerance and sexual deviation. The most debilitating of all emotions may be added to the list: fear, guilt, grief, self-hate and depression.

When any of the above become more of a habit than a normal human response our dreams will target them.

It is the life purpose and mission of every human to develop at least one positive quality in each lifetime.

Our dreams, as directed by our Higher Self, remind us of this and attempt to empower us by (a) helping us to develop the positive quality and (b) drawing attention to the consequences of its negative counterpart in terms of unhappiness, ill-health and non-effectiveness. As is outlined in subsequent chapters, this is the same negativity that creates cancers, heart disease and other serious ailments.

Personal performance in previous lifetimes has a lot to do with the positive quality or qualities we need to develop this time around and each of us has a different avenue to follow. The cruel tyrant in one life becomes a sensitive victim in another and, in the process, is afforded the opportunity to develop compassion. A war-mongering soldier becomes a policeman and, by keeping the peace, can bring that quality on himself. Physical disabilities, such as a stammer, in this incarnation may be 'arranged' to curtail a previous arrogant nature and so foster humility.

In your dream the masculine aspect and its associated qualities are often indicated as something to the right of your vision. This includes the right hand or arm, the right-hand fork in a road or the right shoe. Similarly, the feminine aspect is illustrated to the left. If, for example, your left shoe is missing or stolen apply Rules Three and Four to see what you are trying to avoid in the female side of your nature. This is what you need most in life whether you know it or not.

Apart from the personal quality there is another goal to which we are all expected to aspire. This is 'oneness of mind' which means getting our conscious and sub-conscious minds into harmony with that of our Higher Self.

Our Higher Self sent us onto this planet and makes its wishes for us known through dreams – the Secret Language of the Soul. Such is the perversity of human nature that we resist this as strongly as we try to avoid addressing the personal positive quality. Yet it is only in developing this mental harmony and positivity that we can hope to reclaim some of our lost power.

We first came to Earth as powerful creative spirits possessing God-like qualities with oneness of mind and intent. Negativity and diversity of mind disempowered us. The mind and emotions were scattered in many different directions and, like an army divided against itself, we became powerless. Our dreams try to re-empower us by drawing those scattered elements together in such a way that when we once again achieve our potential we will use it in a positive, rather than negative, way.

The extent of this mental conflict is seen in dreams where we refuse offers from our Guides. They appear as positive people in positions of authority yet our response to them is usually as hostile as our attitude to the Healing Agents. We reject their offers or transfer our 'hangups' onto them to change their appearance and character. They offer us power and we throw them out.

Initially these offers are made, in our dreams, in a kindly and pleasant manner. The gifts are literally offered to us on a silver platter – or gold if one happens to be a healer. If we continue to dig our heels in and stubbornly refuse to co-operate we are reminded of the contract or commitment we made in spirit prior to birth in this incarnation. This is an agreement to (a) undertake certain work or activity and (b) to develop an agreed positive quality in the process. However, what seemed like a good idea on the spirit plane can come into conflict with earthly conditioning and the conventional values of society. In this case our dreams become less pleasant as they insist we remain faithful to our original mission. Further resistance will induce even the most strident dreams and, finally, nightmares, that indicate how this negativity and resistance will eventually lead to the dreamer's illness and death.

Scenes of conflict, war, and destruction, will become a nightly occurrence until we come to our senses and ask, 'What does God want of me?' Your dreams will tell you.

DREAM SEGMENTS

Location and Puns

Absolutely everything in your dream, without exception, is divided into three groups: (a) Things to heal the dreamer (positive), (b) Things to guide (positive), and (c) Expressions of the dreamer's negativity. These apply to the people, children, animals, plants, places, objects, colours, activities and puns which appear in dreams. It is as simple as that. The negative things, and the extent to which positive things become negative as a dream proceeds, indicate aspects of ourselves which need attention.

In order to successfully interpret dreams we need to break them up into relevant segments or components, study each, then re-assemble them into the complete picture. Each segment contains important information in its own right but can only contribute to supplying the full message contained in your dream when its meaning is joined with that of other components. In this chapter we consider two of these as in Location and Puns.

Location

This is the first and most important segment because, in the activity associated with that place, it reveals (a) Subject matter (b) The dreamer's state of mind in present time (c) Cause, as in Cause and Effect.

This information is vital as it forms the basis of interpretation.

It helps if we look on dreams as codes passing from one part of the mind to another rather like the ciphered messages passing between military camps in wartime. Such communications would make little sense to the enemy without the key. Any deciphering expert will tell you it is easy to break a code if you know the subject matter of the communication.

Once you have decided what the subject matter is then everything happening in and around it refers to that subject. All the characters who come into the location have something to say about the subject and positive characters will attempt to heal or give advice on the same subject.

One of the most intriguing aspects of dream interpretation is rebirthing or the expression of the birth imprint on dreams. The most obvious examples of this are when we find ourself in small claustrophobic places like caves where we must scramble towards the entrance/exit before the water rises too far. Or we are in a small room without a door with, perhaps, the walls closing in. We may even be in a narrow hallway, passage, lift shaft, telephone box, toilet cubicle, bus or railway station or the arrival terminal at an airport. All of these locations indicate the birth canal.

A rebirthing dream can also be recognised through a situation where we, or others, approach a building of any kind, enter, meet and interact with the occupants and/or leave again. A large percentage of all dreams involve such a scenario.

The following reference guide is a list of the more usual dream locations.

Airport – Departure – New project, arrival – Birth.

Arena, War, Scene of conflict – At war with yourself.

Art Gallery – Ideals.

Back Garden – The past, Colon, Elimination.

Bank – Energy, Sharing, The heart .

Bedroom – Sex, settlement, Meditation, Astral activities.

Bathroom – Puritanical attitude, need to cleanse the blood, Action of liver and kidneys – especially if there is trouble with BATH, SINK etc.

Boutique or **Carpark** – A choice of roles or attitudes.

Bridge – A need to be 'at one' with yourself, Needing to harmonise your male and female aspects.

Cemetery – Despair, or Change.

Church – Spirituality, Idealism, Philosophy of life.

Cinema – Expansion as in broadening your vision or philosophy of life.

City, particularly the **Capital** – The mind.

Cold Country – Emotional coldness.

Corridor or **Landing** – Transition, Lack of commitment.

Court Room – Judging yourself.

Dentist – Healing of your aggression or bite, animal instincts.

Dining Room – Communication, Inter-action and/or its effect on digestion.

Downstairs – Physical, Emotional .

Driving or **Moving Upwards** – Rising towards ideals, Activating the mental/spiritual aspects.

Driving with a **Family Member** – Carrying the influence of the family: To **Crossroads** – Heading for trouble and/or suffering.

Farm, Countryside – Instinctive, Sexual, Emotional aspects.

Flying – Telepathically leaving your body, Travelling to and from the Astral plane or Rationalising a problem from a more objective viewpoint.

Flying Down and **Landing** – Rebirthing or Practical application of an idea.

Football Pitch – The Game of Life.

Foreign Country (If larger than your own) – A need to expand your awareness.

France – Sexual liberation.

Front Door or **Hall** – Vagina, Birth canal.

Front Garden – Facing life or how we perceive the future.

Garage – Healing of the body.

Germany – Arrogance, Regimentation.

Grave or **Tomb** – The stomach (storage of dead meat).

Green fields – Healing, Harmony, etc. (See 'Colours'.)

Hairdresser – Change the way you think.

Holiday Scene – Relaxation, a need for rest.

Home (room not specified) – How your state of mind was influenced by your family.

Hometown or **Place of Origin** – Influences from the past, Birth.

Hospital or **Doctor's Surgery** – How your state of mind influences your health or healing.

Hot or **Latin American Country** – A need for passion or emotion in your life.

Hotel – The reception at your birth, healing the affect of birth.

Jewellery Shop – Spiritual values.

Journey by **Boat** or **Train** – The dreamer's life.

Kitchen – Digestion, facing the day, Rebirthing.

Library – Your inner wisdom, Knowledge.

Moving Downwards – Going towards the physical/ emotional birth: To the **Left**– Female aspect, emotion or past: To the **Right** – Male aspect, intellect or future.

Narrow Road – A narrow state of consciousness.

Office, Roof or **Attic** – The mind, intellectual attitude.

Old World setting (as in castle, cobblestone courtyard, period costumes, etc.) – Past life influences.

Opera – Expressing emotions.

Post Office – Spirit mediumship, Channelling .

Prison or former **Iron Curtain** country – Repression.

Public House – Social contact, Blotting out sensitivity/ emotion.

Railway Station, Going In and **Out** of a **Building, Going through a GAP** – Birth.

Road running parallel to a river– Your spiritual path, philosophy of life.

Room or Place with Spouse, Partner, etc. – The nature of the relationship.

School – Learning about yourself with a view to improving yourself.

Seaside – Your approach to spirituality or life.

Shop or **Supermarket** – What you actually need, think you need, your accountability, digestion.

Slaughterhouse or **Abattoir** – Self destruction.

South Africa – Extremism – 'Black and White' attitude

Telephone Box – Telepathy.

Theatre – On stage – Performance anxiety. In the audience – Looking at life.

Toilet – Elimination of ideas or emotions, The elimination system.

T-Junction – Choices ahead.

University– The gift of wisdom, higher knowledge.

Upstairs– Mental, and Spiritual aspects.

USA – A need for independence, energy, new ideas.

Wales – Balance (situated in the centre of these islands).

Wedding– Uniting your male/female aspects, marriage or partnerships need healing.

Windows – The eyes, our viewpoint.

Workplace or in **Traffic**– Your work or working on yourself.

Countries and locations can also be divided between 'I am' and 'I need' e.g. *I am*: cold, clinical Switzerland. *I need*: warm, romantic Italy. And so on.

A dreamer cannot rationalise so you might find yourself talking to a tea-pot or listening to a table and it does not seem odd to be doing such a thing. However, even though we cannot rationalise we are still at liberty to exercise free will and can accept or reject the healing and/or guidance it offers.

The following dream will explain further: It takes place in a bedroom. The door of the bedroom opens and a negative old man appears carrying a black dog in a cage. Another character then appears who is known to the dreamer as being kind, patient and sexually liberated. He gets into bed with her and they initially relate to each other At this point the newcomer's face changes to an evil leering grin and he suddenly seems menacing. She is terrified and runs from the room.

Interpretation: The location – subject matter – is the dreamer's sexuality – bedroom.

The dreamer's father – negative male – caused her to fear her own sexuality and, as a result, she repressed her natural instincts – black dog in cage. The second character gets close to her – the Healing Agent sharing his good qualities. The change in the newcomer's face means the dreamer is transferring her fear of her father onto the Healing Agent. She runs from the room – chooses to spoil/avoid the healing effort .

No two dreams are exactly alike but it is fair to say that the majority are a variation on this theme. Basic ingredients are: the dreamer is put into a healing scenario; is asked to face his or her own negative ideas/emotions in relation to the subject matter; Healing Agents get close and offer various types of healing; conditioning prevents the dreamer from accepting the healing by changing the character of the Healing Agent and/or running away.

The remainder are a form of guidance and, as with healing dreams, follow a definite pattern.

Here is an example: The dreamer is in a post office in Soviet Russia. A postman appears and silently hands the dreamer a bundle of letters. The dreamer protests and refuses the offer.

Interpretation: The location, a post office, is the key to the dream in the same way that the bedroom did in the previous dream. The postman is a Guide since he is an authority figure. He chooses to appear as a postman to illustrate the spiritual gift of the dreamer which is channelling or spirit mediumship. By offering letters to the dreamer he is symbolically asking him to be the instrument, medium, or middleman, between those in spirit and those on Earth who request or need information and guidance. The dreamer's reaction is typical.

To understand what different locations mean we must learn to look at ordinary situations, people and objects, in a different light. Only by thinking like a child or a visitor from another planet can we appreciate the symbolic meaning behind the mundane. For example, if you had to explain its purpose to a child or an alien from another galaxy, who never saw or heard of a post office, you would probably say, "a post office is where communications from one party are received, sorted and passed on to another party".

When Rule One – 'Everything is Me' – is applied we see the post office as an aspect of the dreamer. The fact it is situated in Soviet Russia indicates the dreamer has repressed or imprisoned this.

The basic ingredients of guidance dreams are: The dreamer finds himself in a situation which illustrates his spiritual potential: His fears/reservations about developing this potential are illustrated: A guide in the form of a person in authority appears and makes an offer or gives advice: The dreamer, because of his conditioning or lack of awareness, refuses the offer.

Dreams are rarely as simple as the previous examples. To complicate matters a Guide can be a Healing Agent as well.

Consider these locations: If your dream takes place in the front garden the subject matter is going to be about facing the world or the future. A dream taking place in the back garden, your home town or place of origin, it is about influences from the past.

A kitchen is where we make preparations to face the day – or to face life. It is also the place where food is prepared and digested so the subject matter may be the digestive system – and the effect of one on the other. Like how fear of facing life or 'digesting' new ideas affects physical digestion.

If a dream takes place in the toilet the subject matter is going to be elimination – usually of negative out-moded ideas or emotions. However, if the dreamer goes into details about the toilet bowl itself then the physical process of elimination becomes the subject matter and how failure to release the past affects the colon.

Sometimes a dream will move from one scene to another. Ordinarily this indicates two separate dreams but we must consider the connection between the two.

Take the case of the woman who had the following dream. She found herself in bed with her lover. He got up to go to the toilet and, as could only happen in a dream, took off his penis and left it on the bed. She picked it up and started to eat it. At this point she woke up.

Interpretation: The location of the dream – the bedroom – tells us that the subject matter is her sexuality or, to be more exact, her sexual appetite. The man's negative role shows us the effect her father had on her in that her sexuality is of the male aspect only – i.e. detached from emotion. The man detaching his penis further emphasises this idea. The dreamer and her sexuality are put into a toilet as a form of healing – the idea being to eliminate a negative attitude to sex.

The location therefore gives us not only the subject matter but also the dreamer's state of consciousness in relation to that subject matter. This is very important because it is the starting point – the cause of her problem. She has a totally male or macho approach to sex.

The importance of the location of dreams cannot be over-emphasised. If the bedroom is narrow it indicates a narrow approach to sex. A dirty floor points to the dreamer's understanding of sex – it needs to be improved or updated.

Any life problem in relation to sexuality, health or anything else will be referred to by the location of a dream and the details or exact description of that location, particularly if negative, will provide the cause. This always begins with the dreamer's state of consciousness in relation to the issue involved – the way we think influences the way we feel. This, in turn, affects the physical body as, in the former examples, the sexual response.

Puns

Puns may seem trivial in dream interpretation but they are not to be underestimated. A pun will help pinpoint the essence of a dream.

An example of this is a dream which took place at a campsite where two tents had ropes pulled tightly and pegged into the ground.

Interpretation: The pun indicates the dreamer was too tense – 'two tents' – emphasised by tension on the ropes.

Nervous tension is often symbolised by tight ropes, strings or wires. The campsite (pun, a 'calm site') location of this dream is an attempt to bring relaxation – healing – into his life. One can be excused for wondering why dreams contain puns rather than everyday language. The answer is in the sub-conscious mind. Our dreams are, by necessity, in a language and format acceptable to our subconscious which is expected to reply to the message. This is a two-way communication. Dreams are interaction between our Higher Self, which is All wise, All Knowing, and the computer-like subconscious which can only reply according to its programming.

Secret Language of the Soul cannot easily be translated into a spoken form in that it is a universal means of communication consisting of symbols and pictures to which all humankind, regardless of race, colour, creed or technological development can subscribe. Some superficial variations will occur according to the lifestyle of the dreamer – a primitive tribesman is unlikely to dream of telephones, trains or television although the same basic symbols and rules of interpretation will apply.

Spoken language has less meaning for the subconscious which plays around with words without understanding their meaning. It makes 'pictures' instead to avoid mistakes in interpretation – hence the puns.

A story about a computer will illustrate this more clearly. The Russians invented a programme which, they claimed, would instantly translate English into Russian. The phrase, 'The spirit is willing, but the flesh is weak,' was keyed into this modern miracle. The translation appeared as, 'The vodka is good, but the meat is bad'.

And so it is with puns and the subconscious.

CHARACTERS AND ROLES

If everything in a dream is there to heal, guide, or express the dreamer's negativity, then the characters who appear and the roles they play, are of great relevance. Regardless of how many people are in a dream their choice of role is limited to three – The Healing Agent, Guide, or Shadow Self (Negative Role). Although these are usually played by other people it is possible to play the roles yourself.

The Healing Agent

He or she embodies all the qualities that need to be developed in the dreamer. If, for instance, you are fearful or timid your Healing Agent will be courageous or powerful; if you are miserable and pessimistic, the Agent will be happy and positive.

This friend, who may manifest as someone known to us in real life, invariably gets into close contact with the dreamer. He or she might wrap comforting arms around us, share our meal or bed, or simply listen to us. By getting into close contact with our Healing Agent some of those sought after qualities will 'rub off'.

Another aspect of the Healing Agent is that he or she will usually have the qualities that either of our parents lacked. If we dream about a happy carefree woman, it could mean that mother was the opposite. Similarly, a strong decisive man may indicates a lack of such qualities in our father.

A Healing Agent may perform an operation on you. Here the emphasis is less on the qualities he or she has and more on the positive effect of the actions. If he or she appears as a surgeon who is cutting a hole in your head you may find yourself 'opening up' to new ideas!

The efforts of a Healing Agent will be hindered by the dreamer subconsciously transferring negative thinking. This changes the Agent's character or appearance and even the healing effect of his presence.

The following dream was described by a young man who had left a number of jobs for no apparent reason: 'The manager of the Irish soccer team was in charge of a team in which I played. He was helpful, relaxed and supportive (everything the dreamer's father was not). A game was in progress and the dreamer kicked the ball towards the opponent's goal. Although this was a great opportunity to score he made nothing of it. The manager remained relaxed and calm, blaming nobody. Later on he seemed to change and refused to let the game continue when rain came.'

Interpretation: The subject here is the game of life. The dreamer felt he had disappointed his father and lacked his approval (not scoring the goal). He opted out of business life and became a 'fair weather' player.

Note how he transfers his own negativity onto the Healing Agent (the manager). Round or spherical objects symbolise ideals. Those dreams taking place on a playing field often refer to pursuing an ideal (goal-seeking).

The Guide

The Guide, like the Healing Agent, can be either male or female, plays a positive role and appears as a figure of authority. A police officer, teacher, bus conductor, waiter, or any person who speaks or acts with authority in our dream, is a Guide. Sometimes they remain silent and indicate by example what they want us to do. We may even find this role is played by a disembodied voice such as that on a loudspeaker or voiceover on television.

Unlike a Healing Agent, your Guide will avoid close contact and remain remote, though kind and tolerant. In a dream you will find he or she is generally positioned directly in front of you, to the right, or overhead.

These are the symbolic positions from which a Guide can exert the maximum positive influence although if your Guide is female and she moves to your left it indicates she is asking you to activate the female side of your nature.

The occupation of the Guide is highly relevant. A teacher, transport employee, government leader, president, member of religious hierarchy, queen, pope, or Virgin Mary at Lourdes indicates responsibility for movement of the masses in a psychological or spiritual way. The appearance of a Guide in this or a similar role suggests one has power to influence groups of people.

The advice or guidance given will always be correct. None of the other characters in a dream can claim this infallibility but, naturally, you must be sure you are interpreting your dream correctly before acting on it.

Like Healing Agents, our Guides will change character and appearance if we 'dump' our negativity onto them. Finding the Key Words will help here. An authority figure who appears with a physical disability, is drunk, wears black or behaves in an unhelpful manner, is not an indication of a defective Guide but, rather, that an aspect of our own negativity is getting in the way of communication. A limp, for instance, points to the dreamer's inability to move without difficulty (mental rigidity), our refusal to see a point makes them 'blind' and our negativity dresses them in black.

Please remember what you see in a dream is not real in the accepted sense of the word. It is, rather, a fantasy made up of awareness and memories of what was once real. Scattered recollections of the events of the day, the dreamer's youth, birth, and former incarnations are reconstructed to form the learning and healing experience we call a dream.

Our Guides, however, are real and they exist in the non-physical reality we call the Spirit Plane. They are Guardian Angels or 'professional experts' whose main concern is that we persist with our agreed life purpose. We also have many friends and relatives in the Spirit Plane who are concerned with our welfare.

In the deeper levels of sleep we do not dream but instead telepathically leave our body and go to a place or state of awareness which is like a halfway house between Earth and the Spirit Plane. This is the Astral Plane. Here we can meet our Guides and friends, both living and 'dead' and telepathically interact with them to heal, counsel, console each other and share in accordance with our abilities. The dreamer also receives healing and guidance on the Astral Plane. However, in common with Earthly life and the dream state, we also have free will on this level and can choose to co-operate or not.

Our dreams are, to some extent, a re-enactment of the healing and guidance we experience on this level. Memories of our Astral activities are woven into the fabric of a dream. A Guide who had no shape or form there is given the appearance of an authority figure, and friends who healed us appear as Healing Agents, in our dreams.

Sometimes in the course of these interactions we acquire information regarding other people or coming events. These psychic titbits or predictions can appear in our dreams in an unexpected way. Perhaps the dream will reflect a meeting we had with a recently departed loved one. The person may appear silent and smiling in our dream because the communication was telepathic.

It is important to understand the nature of the relationship we have with our Guides. If dreams contain wisdom, healing, and guidance, which comes from our conscience or Higher Self, it follows that a Guide represents and acts on behalf of that Self. How one appears in a dream, and how we react to it, helps us to understand this mutual relationship.

A Guide is concerned with our life purpose, spiritual and psychic gifts, our talents and potential and helps us to develop and use that potential for the benefit of ourselves and others. They help us to progress in spiritual development and to see that, as a soul evolving through every race, colour and creed over a series of lifetimes, we are developing and improving our awareness.

Sometimes a Guide will appear at entrances and ask pertinent questions before allowing the dreamer to enter the next room, meadow or country (the next stage of spiritual development). Or they will offer a symbolic gift such as gold, silver or a precious object (the dreamer's spiritual gift or talent) or the offer might be a proposal to work on yourself or for humanity. As we still have free will in the dream state we are at liberty to reject these. By accepting we heal and grow. Rejection means we refuse an easy way towards spiritual development and may have to learn our lessons through ill-health and misfortune.

The Shadow Self
(or Negative Role)

This third role is negative by nature. The characters will either be unhelpful, cruel, domineering or obstructive, with a thoroughly unattractive appearance and a negative stance. Or the character will be presiding over a scene of destruction and mayhem without displaying any outward sign of negativity.

The Shadow Self can be a male or female and invariably shows the effect the appropriate parent had on the dreamer. If, in your dream, your mother or father comes to visit and finds your kitchen or toilet in a filthy state of housekeeping chaos she or he may appear to be an innocent onlooker but in the dream is, in fact, the symbol of the cause (as in Cause and Effect) of your digestive or elimination problems.

If a negative male character appears as rigid and controlling then one's father may have been like this. Has the dreamer imitated his behaviour or gone the opposite way? Perhaps he lacked control and the dreamer reacted by becoming over-disciplined? Or even timid? A negative male character shows the effect our father had on us. In the same way a negative female indicates mother's influence – particularly on our emotions.

An elderly Shadow Self, represents old, out-moded ideas. A soldier represents regimented thinking, prisoners represent lack of freedom to think. The list is endless. Again, look for Key Words of limitation or containment and list under 'I am'.

Characters dressed in old-fashioned clothes or in a period setting indicate aspects of ourself that we have carried on from one or more former lives. If these people are acting in a negative way it is time to end the cycle but if they are in positive roles – as in helping other people – then the talents we have used in former lives must be reactivated and used without further delay .

The title 'Shadow Self' is appropriate because this is an aspect of ourself with the 'shadow' (or effect) of our parents on it. It may seem unfair to attribute all our negativity to parents but it is a fact that, however unwittingly, they are the main contributors.

Even if we are abused in early youth by people outside parental control we still blame dad for not protecting us. Resentment at this neglect, whether real or imagined, anger at the pain and difficulties we may have experienced at birth, or unpleasant memories of our present parents as we knew them in former lives, all form part of this shadow which can hang over us like a pall.

When dreams present us with the darker side of our nature our initial reaction is usually denial. We cannot believe we are as depicted by this negative character because he or she represents an aspect of us that we want to hide – even from ourselves. Nevertheless we cannot move on until (a) we accept it and (b) we decide to change.

In freeing people from the limiting effects of parents I have found the meditation described in the book 'Cutting the Ties that Bind' by Phyllis Krystal to be very effective. The meditator visualises a circle of golden light all around him or her on the ground. Its radius is large enough to contain the arms when outstretched. A second similar circle surrounds the parent to form the figure '8'. A blue light then negotiates the figure '8' in a clockwise direction, like a toy train on a track, and 'takes away' the the negativity from the meditator. Sometimes, in true dream-like fashion he or she can see this rubbish like tar, cobwebs, or grey clouds, being drawn out and away. Persistent meditation on this over a period of weeks can work wonders.

Children

Children represent aspects of ourselves which are in need of growth. In our dreams a young girl helps to heal or develop emotions, the instinctive or intuitive side of our nature, while a boy helps with individual or creative thought.

Children in dreams mean hope for the future, our responsibility to develop our life purpose, and a zestful approach to life. When the First Rule of dreams – Everything is Me – is applied to children, we see our hopes for the future, our responsibility to develop ourselves and the need to bring new enthusiasm and modernity into our life. Looking at children in this positive way we see that, as with everything else in dreams, they are there to heal and guide. Their guidance often refers to developing spiritual or psychic gifts of which we are not aware or are in the embryonic stage of development.

How do we know what psychic or spiritual gifts we are being asked to develop in ourself? If the child is wearing or carrying precious metals or gemstones it shows the dreamer is spiritually gifted in some way.

A new-born displaying an extra sense like a third eye (indicating clairvoyance) an extra-long nose, large beautiful ears, or wearing earrings, or is otherwise developed beyond his age in terms of expression, speech, or physical ability, indicates you are gifted in psychic or spiritual matters, .

Dreaming of a male child indicates some aspect of the dreamer's masculinity needs attention. This usually indicates a need to develop individual or creative thought but may also refer to any part of the male aspect which needs work. The dream location helps to identify the subject.

If the child is female the emotions, or some aspect of our

femininity, needs to be advanced. But what does it mean if our dream child is negative or badly treated by the dreamer or someone else? The sub-conscious reacts to positive influence from the Higher Self by expressing doubts, fears and reservations. It attempts to limit the development with negativity and shows the juvenile in a limited capacity.

If, for example, we forget to feed – or otherwise neglect our dream child – it is an indication of what we are doing to our life purpose.

Children in negative roles indicate an emotional immaturity existing in present time but with roots in past trauma, usually at the age of the child shown. This is often referred to as 'the child within' – an aspect of our emotions which never 'grew up' or kept pace with intellectual development.

A person in this situation need not be surprised to dream of children under stress, causing trouble, driving cars into danger, breaking things and generally getting into mischief. The dreamer is being shown how emotional immaturity can create havoc with life.

It is also quite common to find negative children in dreams concerning the dreamer's marriage or partnership. This indicates some problems within the relationship may be caused by immature emotions. Even cartoon characters are introduced in dreams to further emphasise this.

Emotional immaturity can be brought about by pain or trauma at birth or in early childhood or as a combination of this and of parents who inhibit the child's development through overprotection, smother-love, anxiety, negativity or passing on their own fears.

Dreams involving negative children will, by highlighting Cause and Effect, illustrate what happened in the past and the repercussions in the present and future. For such a traumatised adult to grow and mature it is vital that 'the child within' be treated. Buried pain from the past needs to be temporarily brought to the fore again, recognised for what it is, and healed. This type of healing is often attempted within the activities in dreams.

A woman told me she had dreamt of a little girl, aged about seven, watching a funeral cortege pass by. There was some sort of break-down or difficulty with the arrangements and the child pushed the coffin up a hill to the church.

Interpretation: The dreamer was, in waking life, molested at that age and suffered a nervous breakdown (the break down of the cortege). She repressed the memory of that incident but with the help of this dream brought it back to conscious awareness. We can see, from the events depicted, the dreamer's determination to put the past to rest in order to mature.

Death and rebirth or rejuvenation is a recurring theme in dreams and it indicates how all growth – physical, emotional, intellectual and spiritual, depends on death of the old self and acceptance – or birth – of the new.

Juvenile Healing Agents who initially enter the dream in a positive way are inclined to be mutated by negative conditioning of the dreamer's sub-conscious, just like their adult counterparts.

A man came to me for advice. Although only in his late Forties he was having memory lapses and blackouts. He came from a large family, had always worked for a large organisation, and was very comfortable with organised Church routine. In all these institutions and with the further inclusion of his marriage he was content to be told what to do or even what to think.

He had a dream which began in a thatched house where he was born in the South of Ireland. In his dream he was in charge of a twelve-year-old mentally retarded boy. The boy had to be taken on a regular basis to Drogheda – a large town in the north which is noted for cement manufacturing. The man who was to transport them had a reputation for being an extremely fast driver but was late arriving. As time passed he became more and more anxious. The child had to be in Drogheda by a certain time. He wondered if they would meet the deadline and if the fast driving would injure the child.

Key Words: Thatched (roof), Mentally retarded, Cement, Late.

Interpretation: Two locations are mentioned in this dream – where the dreamer came from and where he is going, in other words past and future.

The male child is an attempt to get this dreamer to develop individual thought or initiative (his male aspects). He came from a thatched house (pun for attached i.e. lack of detachment or individuality). The activity of the dream also tries to heal this by fast (upward) movement of south to north (activation of the mind). If the movement was from north to south (downward) it would activate the emotions.

The dreamer's subconscious intervenes by portraying his individuality as a mentally retarded boy and preventing the speedy Healing Agent from appearing on the scene (Rule Three). He needed a fast-moving Agent because, in waking life, the dreamer is very slow to move or exert himself.

In reality, this man's father was not there when he needed help to develop this aspect of his masculinity and the age of the child shown is consistent with the age a boy tries to assert his individuality. If this dream shows past, present and future, what is in store for this dreamer if he continues with this activity or, to be more exact, inactivity of the mind? Towns and cities in dreams indicate the mind or the brain while rural areas represent the emotions. The fact that cement is manufactured in Drogheda illustrates how this man's mental sluggishness and habit of allowing others to think for him will eventually lead to brain damage. The cells will 'solidify' or become cemented. Dreams do exaggerate so perhaps this is an over-statement. Nevertheless, when Rule Two – Cause and Effect – is applied and considered the dream implies, 'If you don't use it, you'll lose it.'

Animals, Mammals, Fish and Birds

Animals, like everything else in dreams, provide healing, guidance, and an expression of sub-conscious negativity. Normally they relate to our animal instincts and help us to cope with these instincts and use them in a balanced way.

As an evolving spirit temporarily trapped in an animal body, we are sometimes confused as to what extent we may express our basic urges.

These include survival, sex, aggression, competition, herding, status, feeding, paternity, maternity and affection. Our emotional and physical desires are in common with the lower animals on Earth but, because we carry the memory of sojourns in higher planes, we can have difficulty accepting these basic instincts.

Humankind took music, art and philosophy from the Spirit Plane and introduced them to Earth which, in reality, is the Animal Kingdom and now another challenge awaits. We must strike a balance between our spiritual/intellectual side and the emotional and physical desires of our lower self. In doing so we will further advance our soul .

The animal world is like a refinery or reform school which adds warmth and humanity to cold intellect and ethereal spirituality. Rejecting our animal instincts, as many people do, and trying to live on the planet as a sort of Earth-bound ghost is a waste of time. This ultimately leads to conflict with our Higher Self and the resultant disharmony leads to real physical problems.

The struggle between the physical/emotional and the mental/spiritual aspects of the self is a recurrent theme in dreams. If we are too animal – too much involved with physical and emotional impulses – our dreams will try to strike a balance by getting us to activate the intellectual and spiritual side and vice versa as the need arises.

Rejection or mistrust of our animal nature is shown in dreams by animals playing negative roles. For example, you offer the hand of friendship to a dog and he bites it. When Rule Three – 'I am Responsible' – is applied we realise our own sub-conscious fear of our instincts is creating this apparent treachery. The dog may have entered the dream as a Healing Agent to help us to accept our animality but, as is often the case with Healing Agents, we allowed our sub-conscious objections to get in the way.

Alternatively, we might find, in the middle of a heated argument with others, that we suddenly rise into the air.

Upward movement activates the mind and therefore is allowing us to get an objective view of the situation. The dreamer or Healing Agent might even, for instance, play a role on horse-back to create a balance between the two aspects of the self.

Certain rules must be observed for the duration of our time on this planet. The first of which is to accept the body in which we were born. Many people have difficulty with this and our dreams provide healing by showing animals playing positive roles or meat attractively presented – as in a butchers window. Earthy symbols, like rich loamy soil is another example.

Those who are too timid or are losing a grip of life may

dream about teeth – symbol of animal aggression.

A young man who was undergoing therapy for self-assertion dreamt he was driving his car with an alligator in the back seat. Since this creature is all mouth and teeth he is an appropriate Healing Agent in this case. Unfortunately, the dream ended with the man running from the car.

Losing teeth or fingernails is very common in dreams. This refers to a diminished ability to cope with life due to weakness of animal instincts. If the dreamer is male it indicates problems with libido – many animals assert their right to sex with tooth and claw.

Tomcats are a good example of this as they begin copulation by gripping the female in the back of the neck with their teeth.

Female cats, on the other hand, transport their young to places of safety with the mouth so it is not surprising that women who fear the loss of their offspring dream of losing teeth. Mothers whose families are at an age when they want to leave home often have such dreams. A variation of this is the woman who dreamt of a string of elephants clinging to each other with trunks and tails.

At one of my public talks a woman asked why she constantly dreamt of losing her teeth. I asked if she was aware of a sense of loss in relation to her family. She then told me she had eleven miscarriages and had never managed to bring a pregnancy to full term.

This dreamer needed to accept and develop her animal instinct of maternity to improve her chances of having a family.

It may be difficult to accept that a mental or subconscious difficulty with the maternal instinct can actually cause a miscarriage which is a real physical effect. Nevertheless, it is true that if we humans reject our instincts out of anxiety and try to overly control our body and the subconscious regulation of our glands and hormones we can create actual physical problems within ourself. This is most noticeable with the reproductive system and difficulties can be expected with menstruation, pregnancy, and sexuality if the relevant animal instincts are rejected or limited.

In contrast was a woman who was unable to stop herself having children. As a single parent in a small housing authority apartment she was constantly in trouble because of her growing family. In one of her dreams she was followed by a huge rabbit. It bounded into the supermarket after her, knocking over shelves and causing endless problems. This, rather than rejection of maternity, is over-development or over-indulgence of the instinct, indicating too much animality, and suggests a subconscious need (supermarkets provide for needs) for expression by reproduction.

If a person is too animal, or not animal enough, he or she may dream of going to the dentist. The dentist's function, as the Healing Agent, will be to repair the aggression or bite – indicating the dreamer is not animal enough – or to file down sharp teeth in which case one is too animal or speaks too sharply about others. This type of adjustment or healing may differ on a daily basis depending on the dreamer's daily activity. It may refer to temporary loss of temper rather than a permanent state of aggression.

Problems with sexual potency often manifest as dreams of losing pet animals. One man who had this problem dreamt he lost his dog. When he eventually found it, it had, to his surprise, turned into a little white lamb.

Rule Three – 'I am Responsible' – shows the dreamer was responsible for turning his aggressive sex drive into lamb-like docility. The animals which humankind regard as lowly, particularly if playing negative roles, indicate either what the dreamer has done to his animal instincts or how negatively he regards them.

A man whose family were constantly taking advantage of his obliging nature told me he was constantly dreaming about donkeys and other beasts of burden.

Base animals, such as rodents, are used in dreams to indicate a poor image of the physical body.

A spiritual woman whose upbringing taught her that the physical body was a source of temptation might dream of a rat – symbol of betrayal. If she believed her body was gross a pig may appear.

Remember the location is all-important. If the rat or pig appeared in the dreamer's old family home it was the influence of her family which gave her such a poor impression of her body.

Someone experiencing sexual frustration might dream of cats scraping on the inside of the bedroom wardrobe. The location provides clues as to which instinct is involved.

A positive animal symbol can also give guidance on some occasions. A man dreamt of a cat walking stealthily through very dangerous traffic. Traffic relates to business or career. The dreamer was advised to move carefully in a dangerous situation at work.

Fish usually relate to our spiritual life and expression. Goldfish suggest spiritual healing while the silver variety indicate that the dreamer is more inclined to intuition and flashes of insight. Mutated or distorted fish mean misguided spiritual expression. Any fish trapped in a small pond highlights a need for greater spiritual expansion.

Negative life forms of any kind – especially if they get inside the body and begin growing, gnawing, or eating into the flesh, suggest the threat of cancer.

Here the basic animal instinct of survival is at stake as the body cells grow and develop in an anti-survival mode.

Mammals, such as whales or dolphins, are a species between fish and animals and, as such, are a link between the world of spirit and the animal kingdom. They indicate channelling or spirit mediumship on the part of the dreamer.

Birds, and the colour of their plumage, are also significant. As with animals, mammals and fish, they too are in our dream to heal, guide and express sub-conscious negativity.

If your feathered friend is soaring high in the sky it is a form of guidance – perhaps indicating a goal to pursue? If the goals you choose for yourself are at odds with those of your Higher Self a clash of birds such as hawk vs. dove might ensue.

The following is an example of a bird-orientated dream. A man dreamt he was on a picnic with his girlfriend. As they sat in a field they were surrounded by a circle of day-old chicks – an image that suggested to the dreamer the relationship was immature. That being so, the birds were an expression of subconscious negativity. If, instead of day-old chicks, a series of frozen chickens appeared then it might be said that his emotions were 'on ice' or repressed since 'chicken' is a term of endearment. (Watch for those Key Words.)

Having established the subject matter to which a dream is drawing your attention, the next step is examine the role of your Healing Agent. You are now well on the way to understanding The Secret Language of the Soul.

COLOUR IN DREAMS

In our dreams colour is divided into three categories, healing, guidance, and the dark colours of our shadow self. Bright shades and positive combinations – colours plus white – are a form of healing and guidance. The darker shades and combinations – colours plus black – are a reflection of personal fears and reservations about such healing and guidance.

WHITE The symbol of enlightenment, confidence, perfection, faith, hope and purity. When white is associated or mixed with other colours it purifies and refines their meaning. White alone can indicate a rigid, proud, judgmental immaturity – a 'should-be' perfectionist with a controlling attitude. A soft or pearly white can indicate the gift of prophesy.

BLUE Symbolises our philosophy of life. This includes religion, art, culture, spiritual expression or anything we regard as sacred. If mixed with white the result is a lighter shade of blue. If the healing agent in your dream is wearing light blue, or blue and white, or you are in a room decorated with these colours, you are being guided towards a more enlightened philosophy of life. This is a form of healing.

Darker shades of blue (blue/black) indicate a negative philosophy of life such as an understanding of religion based on fear or the belief that life is 'a valley of tears'.

A nun of my acquaintance who entered the convent because of her (subconscious) fear of life had a dream in which she was running, terrified, deeper and deeper into the convent building. She eventually came to a room where she found a couch draped in blue and white.

The couch, being a cosy and relaxing piece of furniture, was a form of healing asking her to assume an easier attitude to life. The healing colour is white – to give her confidence – in relation to her philosophy. (List under 'I need'.)

A bright shade of blue does not indicate that the dreamer has a positive philosophy of life but rather that he or she needs to develop such an attitude. Blue also has a calming, cooling, effect and is often used to relax and soothe people of an excitable or nervous disposition.

Darker or 'polluted' shades of colour indicate the presence of fear or other negative emotions blocking the healing or guidance. To understand how this works let us consider the colours black and green.

BLACK Represents negativity as in fear, anxiety, hatred, depression – no hope, no faith. When associated or mixed with other colours it adulterates their meaning by creating darker or polluted shades. The same applies to a combination of black plus any other colour. (List under 'I am'.)

GREEN Bright shades of green appear in dreams to heal by allowing us to share energy, to give of ourselves emotionally, and be willing to accept the same in a balanced and harmonious way. This has a healing effect on the heart which requires an inward and outward flow of energy.

Black appearing in the same dream or a dark polluted shade – bottle green or battle dress green – may indicate a fear of sharing or an inability to give oneself to others.

If we cannot share ourself emotionally – constantly taking without giving or constantly giving without taking – the energy going to our heart will be out of balance and may lead to heart illness in later life. These emotional barriers are put up out of fear and 'heart' people are inclined to be over protective of themselves. They have been emotionally hurt in early youth and try to avoid deep commitment in relationships. No one gets close enough to touch their heart. Their dreams constantly put such people into open green areas in an effort to heal.

An example of this was the dream of a man who found himself back in his hometown walking in a grass-covered vacant lot. It was in a rough part of town and, knowing he could be robbed, took the money from his wallet and put it in his shirt pocket. Sure enough, he was approached by four black youths who stopped and searched him. In doing so they touched him all over. As a result of all this intimacy they got to know him and although they found his money they did not take it.

Interpretation: The youths are Healing Agents sent into the dream to help him to share himself. He over-reacts to this healing and sees sharing as a form of stealing. The money is transferred to the heart area – his shirt pocket – in an overly protective manner. The open green area and the youths touching him (pun) are a form of healing. It is his own sub-conscious fears which make them black.

Compare the following dream. It is one of a number in which a forty-eight-year-old man had warning of possible heart illness. In this dream he was working in a petrol filling station on Dublin's north quays. The traffic is normally one-way but in the dream there is a two-way flow. One stream of traffic was much heavier than the other. He was expected to work with his wife and his first duty was to mow the grass margin between the two lanes of traffic.

Interpretation: See the petrol pump as the heart – a solid object – sharing its energy – petrol – with others. The dreamer's wife appears as the female aspect or emotions with which he is expected to work in a harmonious manner. The meaning of the two-way flow of traffic now becomes obvious but note the imbalance. When Rule Two – Cause and Effect – is applied we can see how cause – the lack of sharing – is aligned to effect – imbalance of energy – to the heart.

The colour green in the dream is a form of healing. It is a pleasant, harmonious colour that is a bridge-builder in that it harmonises the male and female aspects. It also opens the heart emotionally.

The healing properties of clear bright green, as the great reconciliator, helps us adapt to conflicts within ourself and with other people, even those with whom we may be at loggerheads. This effect is attempted simply by placing us in green areas on our own or with others. When the colour appears in relationship dreams – those involving a spouse or partner – it highlights the need for adaptability, emotional sharing and generosity.

RED Another colour which is often used to heal relationships. As distinct from blue, which is cooling, red is an exciting colour and will appear in dreams to bring joy and passion into life and romantic liaisons. If this colour appears in our dreams then these qualities may be missing from our lives. This is especially noticeable in dreams concerning themselves with the nature of relationships. If passion is absent the Healing Agent will appear wearing the colour red. This may, or may not, be a current spouse or partner but our reaction to the colour will speak volumes about how much fun and joy there is in our life.

Deep-rooted sexual inhibitions bring a negative response which might take any of the following forms: The dreamer may run away from the Healing Agent or change the Agent's appearance or demeanour; the shade of red may be darkened or tarnished so that it becomes maroon or burgundy; the dreamer may limit or marginalise the colour so that only a stripe remains.

If there is anger or hatred in the relationship, black will appear with the red. Should the combination be one of red and grey then uncertainty or lack of commitment is more likely to be the problem.

A young man who was due to be married had a dream in which he found himself looking into his fiancee's room as she tried on her wedding dress. To his surprise the dress was a shade of grey with a red border instead of being the usual white. This indicated how uncertain and uncommitted he was to the relationship.

The colours a partner wears in a dream indicates your feelings for her or him and not the other way around. The limited amount of red indicates a borderline or uncommitted sexuality while grey indicates uncertainty and the denial of emotion.

Sometimes frigidity or trouble with one's sexuality will be shown as maroon or burgundy – a mixture of red and black – indicating a link between fear (black) – and sex (red). Since the female in the above dream was playing a negative role – the Shadow Self – in that she was displaying a mainly negative combination of colours, it is the effect of his mother on the dreamer which should be looked into. If she (the mother) was uncomfortable or uncertain about her sexuality she may have passed this negative reaction onto her offspring.

Red has a stimulating effect on our creativity, not only in sexual expression and a desire to reproduce, but also any kind of creative work or activity. This can also have a positive effect on our glands and organs associated with the reproductive system. As a stimulant it also helps the heart and the circulation of blood.

Coarser shades of red, such as scarlet, indicate lust, a less refined or more selfish sexuality. Lighter shades (the refining effect of a mix of white and red) symbolise a more enlightened attitude to carnal love.

PINK At the other end of the scale we find pink the colour of compassion, unselfish or unconditional love. Pink is usually associated with mother love. However, if used in dreams as a form of healing it may indicate a lack of this sort of love in our life. We may need to look at how the relationship with our mother limits our ability to give unconditional love to others. Was she able to give love in an unselfish manner? Can we give it to a partner or offspring? If we did not get it we may not be able to give it.

Do not blame your mother if your need for love was not fulfilled. She gave in accordance with her ability. Now the onus is on you to develop and enlarge on what love you have to give to others.

If this is a problem the Healing Agent in your dreams will undoubtedly wear pink, you may find yourself in a pink room, or be offered pink clothes.

To better understand the use of colour in dreams remember to check the following:

* The combination and shade of colours used.
* Who is wearing or bringing what colours.
* Where the colours appear in relation to the dreamer –
  e.g. directly in front, up in the air, or above eye level –
  something to reach for or strive after. Colours seen
  underfoot or below eye level may indicate emotions
  considered beneath you or unworthy of your
  consideration, especially if they are dark or negative.
  e.g. Black and white tiles on the floor – extremism;
  yellow day-old chicks in the toilet – immature fears.
* Is the colour being used to (a) heal, (b) enlighten or
  guide (c) as an expression of sub-conscious negativity?

Consider these points in relation to what we know of
colour so far. Take red, the colour of animal passion, fun,
love, sex, etc.. Animal passion includes aggression, which
sometimes turns to anger, but we may need that aggression,
that willingness to continue the struggle for life, if our
energy or zest for living is low. White, on the other hand, is
hope, confidence, enlightenment, etc.. The healing power of
a combination of red and white in the same dream is clear.

A woman whose 21 year old son was tragically killed in
a fall from a cliff had the following dream: 'I saw my son
standing in the prow of a sailing ship. It had a brilliant
white sail with a red Crusader cross on it and was moving at
full speed before a strong wind. Land was in sight'.

Interpretation: Her son, in this dream, plays a positive role
so he acts as the Healing Agent. The colours he brings are
white for hope and confidence, and red for joy, energy,
courage. Obviously this mother was in great need of such
qualities.

The ship, going at full speed – another healing device – is

'putting the wind back into her sails' while the sight of land is always encouraging. After that dream all the gloom and depression following her loss disappeared. This is typical of the way red and white are used to dispel sadness and despair. Another woman with a very pessimistic attitude to life found herself, in a dream, dancing to music (a healing device) being played by musicians wearing red and white.

In the above dreams the bearers of the colours were obviously Healing Agents but what if the colours were brought by Guides? If an authority figure appears in your dream wearing colours or in a coloured setting he or she may have a healing effect because the Guide can also act as a Healing Agent. At other times, the Guide draws our attention to certain colours to illustrate our spiritual gifts or powers.

If, for instance, you are already, or have the ability to be, a good counsellor then compassion (pink) for the suffering of others coupled with the ability to reconcile conflicting forces (green) are essential to your profession. You may not be consciously aware of these qualities in yourself but if you look at your dreams you may find that the authority figures (Guides) are inclined to wear these colours – often in the form of a green suit, dress or coat, with a pink scarf.

BLACK AND WHITE   When seen together in the same dream indicate an immature, simplistic extremism – a 'black and white' attitude. If something isn't good (white) it must be bad (black). Nothing is that simple in waking life. This perfectionist attitude can cause havoc in relationships because the other party will be judged with impossibly high standards. Naturally, one will be constantly disappointed, angry and frustrated until he or she learns to accept that people are not perfect.

To the black and white person the enemy, or the bad guy, is always clearly defined. If this is your problem then you will dream a lot about black and white objects, people or animals.

Playing football with a black and white ball, for instance, indicates your 'goal seeking' or ambitions are too extremist or simplistic. Perhaps you are judging yourself too harshly and see winning or being first across the line as the only justification for playing the game .

Black and white are a combination of colours that express sub-conscious negativity – maybe a negative reaction to changes proposed to your lifestyle?

The next group of colours to consider are yellow, orange, brown, cream and beige and how they react to black and white in dreams. These colours help us to cope with life in a practical way.

YELLOW Helps us to rationalise. It stimulates the intellect and is especially useful if our problem is coming to terms with fear. When black (fear) is mixed with it the resultant mustard indicates an inability to rationalise or deal with whatever concerns you – being 'yellow' in colloquial slang.

One young woman, a student of my dream course, had a rebirthing dream which indicated that her anxiety dated back to when she was still in the womb. She had picked up her mother's fears. This was shown when she found herself in a little mustard coloured room (the womb). She was terrified of the men who waited for her outside. Then she was greatly relieved to hear that workmen (Healing Agents) were coming to repaint the room a brighter shade of yellow. Yellow (intellect) and white (hope).

If your Guide appears wearing a brilliant shade of yellow you have an enlightened intellect – a mix of white for enlightenment and yellow for intellect. This indicates intuition mixed with a better-than-average intellect which makes one very good at interpreting dreams or any other activity which requires intelligence plus the bright spark of intuition. People with this gift often dream of large high-ceilinged rooms or enlarged head room (enhanced intellectual capacity) in this colour.

Intellectual pride often produces dreams of highly adorned headgear involving bright yellow like the woman who dreamt she was walking in a busy high street. The hat she was wearing carried a beautiful arrangement of fruit, including bananas. She was highly annoyed when people began helping themselves to the fruit. It transpired that, in waking life, she did not like people 'picking' her brains.

Yellow helps us to eliminate in every sense of the word. This includes getting rid of outmoded ideas and emotions and, because the psychology is linked to the physical, the process of defecation.

Our fears naturally affect the digestive and elimination systems. We know this intuitively and refer to a courageous person as someone 'with guts'. Similarly we find that dreams involving yellow or orange often refer to the state of our intestines and our ability to 'stomach' or 'digest' new ideas. It is our fears which hold us to old ideas even when it becomes obvious that these are no longer working for us.

A friend had a dream which disturbed him greatly. It took place in a doctor's surgery (the subject matter will be how his state of mind affects his health). A surgeon (Healing Agent) had cut open his abdomen. Then the surgeon left him lying there, saying that he would call back the next day. My friend was left frantically trying to hold onto yellow-coloured intestinal matter which was falling out of his body. A spacecraft lands and an alien gets out on a tour of inspection. (Key Words: Cut, Hold on, Alien.)

Interpretation: The puns in dreams are highly relevant and this dream is a pun on the words 'being open'. In this case open to new ideas. Old ideas are represented by the yellow intestinal matter. The alien is a new Guide since he comes from another dimension. The dreamer, being a conservative sort of persons, reacts to the new ideas of his guide as 'outlandish'.

Look out for dreams involving the colour yellow, toilets, intestines, courage, letting go or holding on, controlling or accepting, and try to make the connection in terms of Cause and Effect.

Finding yourself in a yellow toilet in a dream means you can be sure that the subject matter is to do with you letting go of anything or anyone who is no longer helpful to your development. This might involve saying good-bye to friends or family members you need to be free of. Such action requires courage on your part because we usually hold on out of fear. Failure to release yourself from anything or anyone as directed by your dreams can result in constipation, blockages in the colon, or more serious problems.

Take a close look at who or what appears in your toilet dreams. They indicate what needs to be eliminated. In the toilet area, there may be rats gnawing into the wall – guilt/anger 'eating you'; naughty children – immaturity; or even ferocious animals – fear. If these represent aspects of yourself of which you need to be free, the colour yellow in the same dream will help you.

Yellow might, on one occasion, heal you by helping the elimination process. On another it could guide you with thoughtful insight into a problem and, on a third occasion, provide a subconscious expression of your intellectual expertise. If the latter is your habitual function and you feel at home operating in this fashion it might not be right for you to develop this thinking, or intellectual aspect of yourself, at the expense of your emotional expression. To correct this imbalance your dreams will introduce other colours to the equation. The healing agent might appear wearing yellow and pink or even apricot which is a pleasant mixture of these colours. This would be designed to bring feeling and compassion into your otherwise cold logic.

CREAM Is the colour associated with acceptance, a growing maturity or a need for tolerance. While I am reluctant to label people it can be useful to know what colour person you are or in other words what is your usual mode of mental/emotional functioning. You can learn this by looking for colour trends in your dreams.

ORANGE Indicates wanting new challenges in life or a need to climb the ladder of ambition. It is not surprising this colour appears in dreams involving career. When this happens its main purpose is to liberate us from repression, or any limiting psychological blockage. This, in turn allows us to take advantage of new opportunities.

When red – creativity – is mixed with yellow – intellect – the result is orange. This helps us to digest new ideas and, naturally, also aids the physical process of digestion. However, if we cannot 'stomach' new concepts and have repressed an adventurous spirit then we can expect to see plenty of this colour in dreams.

Problems with digestion go hand in hand with career difficulties as any ulcerated businessman will tell you. Orange appears in dreams about career and or the assimilation of food.

What we must look out for are symbols which, at one and the same time, illustrate the course of our digestive tract and that of our business or career. Examples of this are dreams in which an orange-coloured mist or fog descended on a train slowly making its way through a tunnel (digestion/career), a slow-moving queue of food consumers at the works canteen to buy orange drink (slow-moving bowel), or sitting at an orange-coloured table at work.

BROWN The colour of practicality. It heals in dreams by helping to earth people who are too much 'up in the air', in other words, those who have difficulty putting ideas to practical use. People who, being of an overly spiritual or other-worldly nature, have difficulty adjusting to the nitty-gritty of every-day life on the earth plane. These will also be healed by dreaming of pleasant shades of brown or more usually combinations of brown (earth), and green (reconciliation).

Some, unfortunately go the opposite way and become too practical or too materialistic at the expense of their spirituality. Their dreams show dull or dark shades of brown as the subconscious expression.

As a spirit functioning on the earth plane all of us require some form of spiritual expression and if we limit this to any great extent we can expect to suffer from depression as these negative shades of brown suggest.

Dark brown (brown and black mix) means we are clinging to materialism out of fear (black) and the absence of faith and hope (white) will naturally bring our spirits down. Dull brown, or brown minus the white of enlightenment, indicates an unenlightened practicality or materiality out of ignorance of any other goal.

An example of this was the case of the woman who dreamt that she met her father at the airport. He was wearing a dull brown jacket and grey trousers. Upon seeing her he turned his back and, without a word, walked up a flight of stairs. She followed him.

Interpretation: This is another rebirthing dream and shows the on-going effect of the dreamer's father apparently rejecting her (turning his back) when she was born. The colours he wears hold the answer to what her reaction was to that first meeting.

When a parent, or indeed anyone playing a negative role, appears in a dull, unpleasant, dark, or tarnished shade or combination of colours, it indicates that we have copied or 'picked up' his or her negativity. Climbing up is aspiring towards an ideal. Following in his footsteps up the flight of stairs is further indication that she accepted his ideals. So, what were those ideals and why were they so wrong for her?

Colours generally reflect emotions. Grey is a non-colour and like black it has no redeeming features. It indicates the denial of emotion. So, her father's dull or unenlightened earthiness (dull brown) and lack of emotional commitment were accepted by her as a role model.

With such a psychological inheritance this woman could never be happy in a relationship and in trying to emulate her father she denied her own femininity by adapting a masculine outlook on life.

As a result of this she separated from her husband, suffers from sporadic bouts of depression, and underwent a hysterectomy.

If a female rejects her femininity the results can be disastrous. The reproductive organs suffer as the awesome power of the subconscious mind is used in a self-destructive fashion. This is usually a result of her father's initial disappointment at the gender of his offspring. To counteract this, male Healing Agents will appear in her dreams wearing pleasant shades of brown, beige or cream (acceptance and tolerance) and red (healing for her sexuality/reproductive organs) If any of these colours appear to those who normally dream of white alone, they are being used to dilute the rigid intolerance suggested by the latter. They will have a softening effect on the immature perfectionism of white. This is common in the dreams of teenagers especially when the delicate subject of personal relationships is in focus.

Blond hair might be described as cream coloured and as a symbol of acceptance it is perhaps the most common and the most effective of all healing devices used in dreams. If, in your dreams, a blonde-haired woman wants to get intimate with you, even if you are of the same sex, you may be sure that she is a Healing Agent whose mission is to bring you a feeling of self-acceptance and tolerance.

If you need to dream of this colour it is usually because mother failed to share those qualities with you at the time of your birth. This would be further confirmed if the blonde woman was also wearing pink – an effort to heal you with acceptance and love. How you react to this therapy is a good indication of how willing, or otherwise, you are to accept these finer qualities in yourself. Tolerance is essential for the harmony of personal relationships. If the healing agent is blond, and/or wearing light shades of brown, this calls for a more mature approach to matters of the heart and to life in general. The Healing Agent will appear as male or female depending on whether you developed the negativity from your father or mother.

Either way an effort will be made to put you into close

contact with the healing effect of these colours in the hope that some of their positive effects will rub off on you. Co-operation with these efforts helps relationships with the opposite sex to be less of a strain.

You may 'dump' some of your negative conditioning onto the Healing Agent. As a result he or she may appear with black hair (fear, lack of trust). This indicates that you do not fully trust men or women as the case may be. The same applies if an otherwise positive Healing Agent is wearing black.

This dream as an example of what I mean: The dreamer, a forty-year-old bachelor boldly walked into a bank and helped himself to money from the cash register. A blonde woman appeared and demanded a share which he gave somewhat grudgingly. He then fell in love with her and they became intimate while still on the bank premises. She gave him an important document or deed encased in a plastic folder.

Interpretation: We know from previous dreams that the ability to share yourself emotionally with others has a bearing on relationships and the heart itself. The location of this one, a bank – in waking life a venue for sharing, or the giving and taking of money – is a popular dream symbol for the heart and matters relating to it. Dreams of females making demands and/or girls at cash registers as one leaves a building usually indicate that mother had difficulty giving herself in an unconditional way. From birth she gave us to understand that we will only be acceptable if we achieve.

We tend to transfer to other relationships the feelings we experienced at the first meeting with our parents. By accepting this demanding attitude as the norm we are less able to give of ourselves. As a result, relationships suffer initially and, finally, the physical heart is weakened.

The blonde woman appeared to help the dreamer in this regard. Making love in public, as he did in the dream, helps him to be more open with his feelings and to bring the male and female side of his nature into a harmonious unit.

A deed is a form of entitlement to a building or property – his body – a way of telling him that he is entitled to be born. Since his mother could not make him feel so at birth the symbol of entitlement is covered in plastic – an unnatural substance.

GOLD , SILVER , PURPLE , and INDIGO
These generally appear in conjunction with Guides and relate to your spiritual gifts.

Gold Spiritual healing, creativity.

Silver Intuition.

Purple (A mix of blue and red) Spiritual power, leadership, spiritual teaching, authority in spiritual matters.

Indigo Clairvoyance.

PATTERNS IN DREAMS

The more we study dreams the more we find that certain patterns emerge. Every chronic illness, for example will cast its distinctive shadow in dreams years or even decades before it manifests in the physical body. By studying these patterns it is possible to (a) predict the illness in time to take remedial action and (b) recognise the personality types who will be more prone to one particular ailment rather than another e.g. the heart personality, the cancer personality and the stroke personality.

The latter's dreams will often feature the colours black and white to indicate his rigid, uncompromising attitude, references to a slow-moving hardened colon and, of course, polluted blood. Sometimes there will be scenes of conflict or accident often resulting in injury as someone's head collides with a cement or stone floor (dreamer's understanding). Basically, this is a form of control (white) based in fear (black) There may also be a history of headaches or migraine.

A man in his forties who periodically suffered from migraine and whose mother and aunt both died from a stroke had the following dream: The scene was a heavy-weight boxing contest between Mohammed Ali and another black man. The dreamer felt that he was Ali. Both boxers wore white shorts so the only colours mentioned were black and white. The dream ends when his opponent knocks him to the ground which, as his head strikes it, he realises is cement rather than canvas. (Key Words: 'I am' Black, White, Strike, Cement, Fight.)

Interpretation: Two men fighting suggest a conflict of ideas (the male aspect). The cement floor (pun) indicates a rigid understanding of life. His opponent's dark colour symbolises a fear of other people's ideas and the resultant injury, as concrete and head meet, are the end result of the foregoing – Cause and Effect. An obvious pun is the final blow (or stroke). This dream alone proves nothing but I mention it because it is typical of the migraine/stroke personality. The usual ending of such dreams is in head damage.

A conflict of ideas in the former example is brought about when progressive new ideas, presented to the dreamer by his Higher Self or Spirit, are challenged by his will or mind. This can create disharmony of body, mind and spirit, an infallible recipe for ill health. In this dreamer's case, a stroke. These new ideas represent an alternative philosophy of life which the dreamer is asked to embrace. However, his fears prevent this and the resulting conflict puts pressure on his brain.

Another example is the case of a young man in his thirties. He had been studying his dreams for some time and their recurring trend was trying to persuade him to open his mind to new ideas. He stubbornly refused to do so until he had the following dream: He was with his year-old son in an open topped, double-decker bus. The child was playing and climbed onto the rail around the upper deck. The father shouted at the boy who, startled, fell to the ground and banged his head on the concrete.

Interpretation: The dreamer was being asked to open his mind (the open top bus) to inspiration and new ideas. The young boy symbolises new ideas. The age of the child, one year, is important as 'one' is the symbol of individualism .

The dreamer was being asked to break free from the limits of convention and to accept guidance from above or his Higher Self. However, a fear of 'going over the top' (losing control of his mind) brings on the conflict. After that dream he became more amenable to change. Similar dreams of colliding cars causing head injuries, or banging a child's head off a wall, are also typical of this type of problem.

When serious trouble is predicted for the digestive tract, such as ulcers, colitis, etc., warning is given in dreams by reference to damage to solid objects such as trains crashing or being derailed. Often it is family pressure to achieve in the area of career that lies behind this.

One man who was a refuse collector put himself under pressure because of what he regarded as the lowly nature of his job. He had a dream in which the refuse truck (his elimination) was on a collision course with a train (his ambition).

The vehicles collided causing great loss of life; his own unless he resolves the conflict inside himself regarding career.

Any kind of tracked vehicle, such as a bulldozer or tank, can be a pun on the digestive tract. The most common example of this is a railway train which can mean any or all of the following: the dreamer's career, course of life, or digestive system.

In many dreams a train refers to all three and how one influences the other. If the dreamer's attention is drawn to problems with the engine, an obstruction on the track, a collision or derailment, it means a health warning. Trains are solid objects used for the transportation of material over a set course so the analogy with the digestive tract is obvious.

Please remember that if a health warning is given Rule

Two will indicate the cause. This is often stress and anxiety in relation to career and/or acceptance through achievement. These problems are generally a reaction to father since he still tends to be the more career orientated member of the family.

Sometimes children grow up with the idea that they will not be accepted unless they achieve. If they doubt their ability to deliver the goods the resultant stress will eventually be reflected in ill health. As I indicated dad is usually the guilty party here, but sometimes it is Mum who was the real driving force as you will see from the following dream.

The dreamer is a nineteen-year-old, Dublin born, female student. She was under considerable pressure to pass her exams when she had this dream: 'I was aware that a nuclear explosion had taken place. My mother was with me and she was telling me to hurry. We made our way to a railway station. A voice over the public address system told us that victims of the nuclear explosion should take the next cattle truck to Dundalk (a city north of Dublin). We boarded the train. It went forward a few hundred yards and then it became derailed'.

Interpretation: When I heard this dream I predicted this woman would develop problems in the digestive tract. Six months later she was diagnosed as having ulcerative colitis – ulcers or sores forming on the wall of the large intestine and, like stomach ulcers, a direct result of stress.

In this instance the stress was caused by her mother's pressure on her to pass exams and get on with a career (being hurried to get on a train). The nuclear explosion represents her emotional turmoil; the cattle truck, transporting meat and presumably manure, her digestion;

the derailment, her predicted illness.

To make predictions, remember to link all the symbols in a chain of Cause and Effect. Cause was mother's pressure and illness the Effect. It is interesting to see another little device used here to indicate the future. When activity is depicted as happening along a road or in this case a railway line, and we are told what happens at a further distance then we can predict the most likely future Effect. What happens down the road or down the line represents what is yet to come. The passage of time is shown as a journey through space.

The healing aspect of the dream is the recommended movement from South (Dublin) to North (Dundalk) which, like movement upward in a dream, has a cooling effect on heated emotions.

Dreams indicate how pollution of the digestive/circulatory systems contributes to many serious health problems but could it also be a factor in cancer? We know that cigarettes, radiation, and animal fats, feature in the creation of this serious illness, but are they the cause? Over the years that I have studied these problems I have been particularly interested in the dreams of those who had already contracted cancer. From this I was able to establish patterns and found that people at risk were being warned in dreams of the possibility of getting the disease.

How does cancer appear in dreams? Cancer is a life form – a distorted or mutated body cell that goes renegade. It grows and multiplies and unless treated or removed will destroy the body.

It appears in dreams as a low-class or mutated animal, insect, living organism or growth form such as a rat, mouse, squirrel, worm, woodworm, rust, etc. The pattern of its growth and multiplication also manifests in dreams.

It might appear as a rat or mouse burrowing its way into the body and growing inside us. Or, as one man experienced, a worm jumping out of meat on the frying pan, falling to the floor, getting in under the cooker and producing young. In his case the vulnerable area would be the digestive tract. Cancer of the colon is common and fatty meat is to be avoided. But is it the cause? It is no more fair to say that cigarettes, radiation, animal fats and pollution cause cancer than to say that bombs and guns cause wars. Wars are caused by reactivating old scores, ancient grievances and hurts that have never been properly dealt with. Bombs and guns are simply handy weapons.

This is also true of cancer. It begins in the mind and emotions, where it remains dormant or semi-dormant for years and then it erupts like a war when incidents in the present parallel traumatic incidents from our birth, early life, or previous incarnations. The resultant hurt and pain eats into the harmony of our body. It is also true to say digestive tract/circulatory pollution is a factor to the extent that it becomes a means to an end. Indeed, if we are not prepared to accept and deal with the psychosomatic dimension to this and other ailments then we should at least think in terms of cutting off the source or supply by ceasing to pollute our digestive and or circulatory system.

DIGESTION, ELIMINATION, ALLERGIES

Because of having a daily bowel movement we may believe ourselves free from intestinal problems. This is not necessarily the case. Waste eliminated on a particular day may already have remained in the body for too long.

This is quite common and, while not life threatening, can lead to pollution within the body if left unattended. Excrement remaining too long in the bowel allows toxins to seep through the walls of the large intestine – the colon – and enter the bloodstream. To stay in peak condition it is necessary to ensure our blood is pure. If you are in any doubt about the length of time it takes your digestion to work get some charcoal tablets from the chemist and take the prescribed dose. Then watch how long it takes the faecal matter to turn black. Any longer than twenty-four hours may indicate sluggish digestion.

The shape and condition of the colon and state of the blood are two of the most common health themes in dreams. Indeed, the humble colon, which is largely ignored, emerges from our dreams as the hub of many health issues. Because we normally only see a colon in medical textbooks, we believe it is a six-foot length of tubing, of uniform thickness, that efficiently carries our waste to the rectum. That is if we think about it at all. In actual fact, as any doctor will verify, most adult colons are far from being regular and uniform. Some sections are twisted and others are squeezed into narrow passages. Waste matter negotiating such cramped areas tends to build up causing the colon to balloon in other sections. The result is a slow-moving bowel.

Scientific analysis of colonic waste shows it can be in the body for up to twenty years, building up against the walls of the colon and hardening to a considerable thickness.

This leaves only a narrow centre for current waste to pass through .

Dr. Harvey W. Kellog, M.D., of Battle Creek, Michigan, said, 'Of the twenty-two thousand operations I personally performed, I never found a single normal colon. And, of the hundred thousand performed under my jurisdiction, not over six percent were normal'.

A distorted colon is not, in itself, a health hazard. The problem lies in the release of toxins seeping out from waste matter. Meat, if it remains too long in the colon, tends to over-ferment and the resulting toxins pollute the blood which must, in turn, cleanse itself. In the process it redistributes the toxins over different parts of the body. If these settle in the joints calcification is the result and can lead to arthritic conditions later. Memory lapses are possible if toxins are deposited in the brain. Further problems can manifest as clogging of the lymph or other glands, skin problems, pollution of the blood or congestion of the lungs. Clogged lymph glands can lead to coronary thrombosis (blood clot) if left unheeded. This condition is portrayed in dreams as dirty green water-logged, swampy, grass.

Polluted blood trying to cleanse itself through the skin because of lymphatic clogging causes boils and other skin problems. This is illustrated in the following dream: The dreamer, a man in his forties, found himself back in that part of rural Ireland where he lived as a child (inability to release the past). He was relaxing along the banks of a canal (the canal network represents his circulatory system) when he noticed that reeds and other vegetation had grown out from the banks into the water (clogged lymph glands). He stopped at Scally's Hotel and decided to stay overnight. In reality, Scally's was a farmhouse he remembered from his youth.

Scally is a common, Irish surname but here it is a pun on 'scaly' referring to the state of the dreamer's skin which from time to time flared up with inflammations.

The building stood on bogland (lymph glands) and every Christmas morning a candle was lit in every one of the nine windows to the front of the house (the face). The glare of these lights is a pun on 'inflamed' which describes his skin – especially after over-eating at Christmas. 'Scaly' would also describe it for the rest of the year. When we apply Rule Two – Cause and Effect – we see it is the undrained, polluted, state of the blood that is responsible for the problem.

Cause usually precedes Effect, even in a dream, so the state of the canal mentioned before the house clearly puts the cause down to the condition of this man's blood.

The colon, as a reflex organ, is very susceptible to emotions. A pattern of fear and nervous tension, beginning in the womb, continues throughout life. Excessive control – holding back feelings due to fear of living, or of sexual or emotional expression, can tense up the colon. This is often shown in dreams as black and white animals – sometimes trapped in a fearful state in a little room (restricted animal expression while still in the womb) or in a threatening situation to the dreamer, as in being chased by black and white bulls. The black (fear) and white (rigidity in this negative context) indicate excessive control. When these colours are used in a dream carrying a health warning it shows that repression of sexual or emotional expression is causing, or likely to cause, problems of the colon and / or blood stream and related areas.

One common problem caused by a slow-moving toxic bowel is the condition, Candida Albicans. This is a fungus growing within the digestive tract which causes numerous side affects including lethargy, depression, loss of sex drive, constipation, etc. It appears in dreams as a reference to musty old rooms, mildew, mould, smell of damp and the like. Such dreams usually take place indoors and, invariably, a toxic bowel appears as the cause.

The colon often appears in our dreams as distorted or twisted-up hosiery, tights, tubing or something of that shape, and polluted blood is indicated as dirty stagnant water. Do not be alarmed by this as the blood rights itself quickly through an elaborate system of cleansing and draining carried out by the lymphatic system.

These hard working glands are situated at strategic parts of the body. If a cut foot becomes infected an obvious swelling may be found at the back of the knee. This is the lymphatic system in action as the gland draws infection away from the cut to prevent it from getting into the blood stream.

Exercise, a change of diet, herbal remedies or colonic irrigation, particularly under medical supervision, will help to rectify any sluggish system. Working up a sweat through physical exertions or a sauna stimulates elimination through the skin and gets the lymph glands working properly.

It is very encouraging to study your dreams while undergoing changes in diet, lifestyle or therapy, because they will monitor your progress.

Food Allergies

Food, the stuff of life, is not always successfully accepted by the body and can produce allergies.

This all starts with the emotions we feel as we take our first meals from mother. If she is angry or fearful (regardless of why) as she breast feeds, the child can sense this and reproduces the emotion in himself. He may link these feelings with the food and, forever afterwards, have a negative reaction to dairy produce.

The body is like a factory that turns food into raw material. From this we create structures and effects that subtly reflect our habitual state of consciousness. Through programming the sub-conscious from birth we create defenses to protect us from what we learned to regard as a dangerous and threatening world.

An infant begins life with enormous fears and needs a massive amount of love and reassurance. We need to know, for instance, that we are safe and the air is fit to breathe. If a mother is unable to reassure her baby on these points the child programmes its sub-conscious mind to use mucous to block the bronchial tubes and keep out threatening air (asthma). If we wish to numb our senses the mucous is used to clog up the sinuses (sinusitis) and so on. Milk, cheese, eggs, other dairy products, and animal fats, are used to manufacture this slime.

Allergic reactions to wheat and other food items begins at a later stage when the child moves to solid foods.

One woman developed an allergy to wheat because her grandmother used to beat her if she didn't eat her porridge. This manifests in dreams where the mother, or negative mother figure, appears and some form of heat (anger) is applied to milk and other items.

The state of the lungs is a reflection of our reaction to life and the world in which we live. If the world is seen as threatening we sub-consciously believe we are not safe in it and may develop lung problems. This appears in dreams as references to machines and appliances that draw in air – or to rooms or cavities in which the quality of the air is mentioned. If they are smoke-filled, or stuffy as in an over-crowded doctor's surgery, it indicates one or both lungs are congested. References to life and living are further clues.

A woman, whose birth was so complicated she was not expected to live, had a rebirthing dream in which she was given a chest massage by a Healing Agent whose name was Olive (a pun for 'Oh live' or 'please live').

Another example is a dream in which a man found himself repairing his vacuum cleaner. In waking life he owned a similar appliance which was red. The vacuum in his dream was grey, flat on one side and rounded on the other, like the shape and approximate size of a lung. The paper bag inside was ineffective. Dust and fluff stuck to the sides of the machine inhibiting its ability to draw in the air.

Interpretation: In cleaning out the dust and fluff the man was trying to clean his lungs. The colour grey indicates lack of commitment to life. This is the cause and weakness of the lung is the effect. In waking life this man had a weakness in his left lung.

Dreams show us how stress and nervous tension – usually about work situations or trying to live up to parents expectations – contribute to the creation of an over-acid or ulcerated stomach.

A man in his forties who was experiencing career difficulties had this dream: he was handed a glass of whiskey 'for punishment'. Instead of drinking it he put his index finger into the glass which caused the liquid to heat up and turn into a fizzy drink. In punishing himself for his lack of career achievement his anger (heat) is turning alcohol into acid in his stomach. Next, he found himself in Westminster Abbey. The stomach often appears as the cavity of a grave since both are used as receptacles for carcasses. Westminster Abbey is a grave site but only for those who have achieved fame. The Queen had offered him a job, but first he had to get on the end of a queue to fill in forms. A queue invariably suggests the digestive system – a line of food moving in the intestines. A nasty, impatient, man was taking details from the people at the end of this rather long queue which had formed on the right. A much nicer person was in charge of another smaller queue on the left.

The dreamer's intolerance of his situation and his poor elimination comes from judging himself with the harshness of his male aspect only – the right. He would eliminate quicker and with greater efficiency if he used the compassionate female aspects of forgiveness, acceptance and letting go – the left queue.

People in the congregation knew that, being unemployed, he was in need so they began to place money in his hands and pockets. This is charity-giving without repayment. He is being asked to be kind and charitable to himself. It is doubtful if this man's parents gave him unconditional love. He could hear the sound of drilling and noticed plaster falling off the interior walls and holes appearing. These holes were, apparently, for steel rods which could hold the crumbling Abbey together. The crumbling plaster work and holes represent sores on the wall of the stomach – ulcers. The steel rods indicate the folly of judging yourself with the male aspect only.

If all this is confusing keep in mind that if the building represents your physical body the stairs which are a column of platforms winding their way up its centre indicate the spine. Leading off from the stairs are usually various rooms – all indicating different organs and systems of the body e.g. the kitchen (digestion), toilet (elimination), living room (circulation), bedroom (reproduction), bathroom (kidneys), front door (vagina), back door (rectum), and so on. Naturally, mention of physical damage within these areas warn of health risks to the appropriate functions. In the above example we can see how the dreamer's reaction to Dad's criticism of him causes him to judge himself harshly (the nasty man in charge of the right hand queue) and the effect this has on his stomach (the interior walls of the Abbey).

If, for example, an unpleasant man appeared on the stairs and the dreamer described steps missing or a rotten, defective handrail then spinal problems such as slipped discs might be indicated and Dad's unsupportive attitude would be a very important circulatory factor to the illness (Rule 2). Dad is supposed to be the 'backbone of the family'. If he is overly critical, weak or unsupportive he can induce physical problems in his offspring who grow up with the idea that they are unsupported. No amount of physical treatment for such ailments will be successful in the long term until the psychological background is addressed.

Dreams can be relied upon as early warning systems to allow the dreamer to enjoy a healthier life. What we die from is a concern, but what we might have to live with may be more of a worry.

THE HEART AND CIRCULATORY SYSTEM

Most people are all too aware that unclean blood contributes to serious heart ailments. One common example of self-induced pollution to the circulatory system is the tar and nicotine from smoking which can, over time, cause hardening of the arteries, clotting, strokes and interfere with the blood circulation with serious consequences.

The lymph glands, liver, and kidneys work overtime to clean, drain, and filter the blood of these toxins before it returns to the heart. This industry is shown in our dreams as references to the waterworks of a house (Rule One – ourself).

A middle-aged woman who was suffering from pernicious anaemia (blood problem) had the following dream: 'I was driving along Dublin's North Circular Road. My car was in a very poor condition with oil from the engine leaking onto the road. I gave a young man a lift and he pointed out the fact that my tyres were deflated. I went to a garage but the (male) attendant there was very unhelpful. He told me to go to the next garage for a certificate and return with it before he would put air in my tyres. My bicycle was also flat.'

Key Words: *I am:* In very poor condition, Leaking Oil (anaemia), Deflated, Flat. *I need:* A lift (encouragement), A young man (new ideas about myself).

The location of the dream – the North Circular Road – difficulty with the wheels and oil circulation all point to the circulatory system and the unhelpful garage attendant indicates how Dad's apparent lack of acceptance of her contributes to her condition.

To simply dream of this or any other of our physical functions does not necessarily mean that our health is seriously at risk. If one goes on an occasional alcoholic binge this will quite possibly appear in a dream, as the liver and kidneys try to cope with the extra alcohol toxins added to the existing pollution. However, repeated references to these organs may be taken as a warning of possible future trouble – while offering the opportunity to avoid it.

Our kidneys are bean-shaped, located either side of the body, and produce urine. Therefore they may be represented in our dreams as the taps of the kitchen sink, two small bottles carried on either side of a coat or jacket, or even as a couple of garden gnomes urinating into a pond.

The liver is shown as any kind of kitchen filtering system such as a sieve or even a plastic basin full of soil or charcoal allowing water or other liquid to filter through it. The key word 'plastic' could indicate the organ was also trying to cope with some unnatural or inorganic substance.

We can only survive putting rubbish into our system if it can be safely and efficiently eliminated. If not, we become terminally poisoned. Sauna, exercise and simply working up a sweat not only eliminate some of the toxins but also help to cleanse the lymph glands. We may be urged to speed up this process by dreams in which we are vigorously riding a bicycle. Reference to a bicycle, a series of wheels, and the figure 8 (or a 3 which is an eight sliced in half) all refer to the circulation of blood.

Such dreams often take place on a road or highway

which may be described as a 'main' or an 'arterial' (pun) road. A road that begins or ends at a roundabout indicates the direction of the circulatory flow. Minor lanes leading into the main highway – particularly if described as muddy – allude to pollution coming from the colon. An unmistakable example of this would be to dream of mud splashing up from a dirt track or lane and getting onto the wheels or chain of the bicycle as you approach the main road.

If we ignore health advice in our dreams and do not bother to cut out polluting practises, or get enough exercise, we may have a warning of our death. This is not a cause for immediate alarm, but at the same time is best not ignored. Such information is simply your dream underscoring something you know already about your lifestyle. Perhaps your doctor has asked you to slow down, stop smoking or drinking alcohol, take better care with your diet or try to get out more.

Dreams are not medical diagnoses and when they refer to physical or mental health it is simply to warn us what lies ahead if we do not change. If you have a health concern, see your doctor.

'Heart' dreams often take place at an apartment (being apart from others). An island or wall, indicates the defensive emotional 'wall'. An example is the man who dreamt he was on Achill Island. His holiday was coming to an end and he was saying goodbye to his girlfriend who was dressed in grey. They walked together as he wheeled his bicycle along a narrow lane leading to a highway. His knapsack (bag) containing brown bread hung on his bicycle. When they got to the end of the lane a No. 83 bus was waiting at a green roundabout.
(Key Words; End, Goodbye, Grey, Narrow, Bag.)

Interpretation: The urgency of this dream is indicated by the reference to death: Achill is pronounced A-kill. So too it is the end of the holiday, the end of the lane and, finally, brown bread – rhyming slang for 'dead'. The bicycle and colour green were healing agencies that tried to bring balance and harmony into his life. The colon was indicated by the knapsack of food and narrow lane. If, as he left the island, the ebb and flow of the tide were uneven or the traffic went more in one direction than another then the 'give and take' (emotional sharing) of everyday life would be a factor. Saying goodbye to his girlfriend indicates how he separates himself from emotion.

Those prone to developing heart ailments can benefit from 'getting a load off their chest' through counselling or by getting into the habit of saying exactly how he or she feels about a situation.

This type of sharing is illustrated in dreams by pouring tea from a teapot (emotional outpouring from the heart) or by a kettle 'letting off steam' (regulating the blood pressure). The teapot or kettle symbolise the heart so sharing a cuppa with a friend is a pleasant example of dream therapy. Other heart symbols might be – a car engine (is the 'oil' circulating through it clean or dirty?), pulling pints of porter at the pub and sharing them with friends, a clock ('ticker' is colloquial slang for the heart), or moving in an 'anti-clockwise' direction (something in your present behaviour is not good or wise for your 'ticker').

Sometimes we humans need reminding that we occupy an animal body. Lower animals tend to live on the edge or in a near-permanent state of emotional excitement. Look at the way some dogs react to a knock at the door! Once contented the danger has passed the pooch stops barking, sits back and happily wags his tail. Should the occasion arise he would be ready for another alarm in a split-second and enjoy it just as much. Animals are emotionally uninhibited and naturally passionate. Most humans, on the other hand, have learned through the rules of polite society to cushion ourselves in case any outward display of emotion might meet with disapproval. This makes life dull, sedentary and pedestrian. Our dreams try to rectify this by placing the dreamer in a hot passionate or steamy setting – a Mediterranean or Latin American country – and/or subjects one to the colours of passion (red) and sharing and balance (green). (Listed under 'I need'.)

These healing agencies might be casually introduced as in red and green traffic lights at a crossroads or perhaps a policeman or traffic warden (authority figure in charge of traffic flow – your blood) may indicate by word or gesture that you are to move or drive to the left (the female or emotional side), to keep moving, or even drive faster to avoid the pedestrian (pun) pathway.

Sometime the healing comes in a more bizarre fashion as with the woman who dreamt she was lying, on her back, on the floor of a spiritual healers house. A woman (Healing Agent) comes through a door in the wall. She is wearing stiletto heels and stands on the dreamer's chest, pressing her heel into the heart area.

Note how this dream 'opened' the wall and stimulated the heart.

The condition of any grass (blood) in your dream is important. This is where the two greatest pollutants, mucous and toxins, will appear. Look for anything white mixed into the grass such as chewing gum, cotton strands, lengths of yarn, soggy paper or papier mache or any white or off-white slime. Bald patches of brown earth, mud or other brown material indicates the presence of faecal toxins. Pollutants in dreams described as brown, white or plastic can be taken to mean faecal, mucous or inorganic toxins respectively. The latter usually refers to chemicals used in the manufacture of certain alcoholic drinks.

Finally, warnings of impending arthritis will also show up in dreams to do with the circulation. This desperately painful condition in which the joints are cemented together, begins with crystalline deposits floating in the blood. These are shown in dreams as crushed glass scattered in the grass and, as with other health problems, the warnings appear decades before the condition manifests.

FERTILITY AND REPRODUCTION

Subconscious conditioning that sex is unclean often provides the basis for problems with fertility and reproduction.

This belief has been created at some time in the dreamer's past and not necessarily even in this lifetime. When a person took vows of celibacy in a convent or monastery (or in secular life as part of some self-imposed penance) during a previous incarnation it can manifest as a sexual problem in this life. The dreamer may even have previously known one or both parents as fellow monks or nuns centuries ago and is, perhaps, now being pushed by them to enter religious life or attain a level of distinction that the dreamer feels is beyond his or her capacity. All of this adds to the conflict and confusion of the individual.

Just as the feminine aspect is indicated in dreams by such symbols as vessels and containers, the masculine is represented by phallic symbols. Damage to, rejection or avoidance of these or similar symbols suggests a weakening of the sex drive and/or a health risk.

Problems in the area of intimacy, potency, and reproduction that appear in adult life may well have begun at birth when a parent is, for whatever reason, unable to demonstrate unconditional love and acceptance towards the infant. A child is telepathically sensitive to its parent's wishes, ambitions and reactions at this point and if it detects any criticism it can have far reaching effects. He or she can learn to turn it inward, to judge his or her self harshly, and if this negativity becomes focused on the genitals – symbols of the child's sexuality – it can be the beginning of a problem that may not openly manifest until the person has become an adult of forty, fifty, or more years.

An extreme case can produce cancer in some part of the reproduction area, whatever the gender of the individual. The following dream illustrates such a situation.

A man dreamt he was taking his parents on a journey and although he had driven for hours, had only reached Boyle – a small town in Ireland. He was anxious to conceal this fact from them. As he drove he crashed into traffic bollards, damaging the wing mirrors of his car, but he did not care. Then he met a policeman whom he thought he recognised. This policeman turned out to be, in the dreamer's words, 'not the man I thought he was'. The scene changed and he found himself playing a round of golf with a colleague who had died some years previously. The men are at the tee box and the dreamer is furiously hitting his golf balls.
(Key Words: Box, Conceal, Damaged, Died, Hitting (Effect), White (Cause). *I am*: 'Not the man I thought'.

Interpretation: The dream indicates the dreamer's subconscious self-criticism and rejection of his maleness – traffic bollards, wing mirrors. Mirrors reproduce an image of the self and can symbolise reproduction. If there had been damage to the door handles it would carry a similar meaning since 'handle' is a pun for name and a man passes on his name to his offspring. Wing mirrors and handles are appendages to the car – the dreamer's body. The golf balls symbolise the dreamer's testicles and the town of Boyle is a pun for 'boy' or 'boy-ill'. People who develop cancer are often seen in their dreams to 'play a round' (pun, 'play around') with death as indicated by the golfing companion.

In fact this dreamer's parents wanted him to become a Roman Catholic priest. In the opening sequence of his dream we can see how he tries to conceal his inability to satisfy their ambition for him to 'go far' in life. Round or spherical objects in a dream represent goals in life therefore the white golf balls in the final scene are, at one and the same time, contending views of his choice of career and/or celibacy. The subconscious, although not intelligent, has awesome power over the body.

It tends to respond to conflicts such as this one in a coldly logical way by removing the 'bone of contention' – in this case the dreamer's testicles – unless he resolves the issue and becomes at one with himself, thereby lessening the risk of testicular cancer.

This particular woman attended one of my dream courses and it was obvious she was an intellectual. Her dream was located in her bedroom situated at the top of the stairs – indicating she has a mental or intellectual approach to her sexuality. She regarded a low or rectangular table in the bedroom as a nuisance and shoved it out of her way. The Latin for table is mensa so the table here is a pun for menses or menstrual system which, with reproduction, is part of a female's sexuality. In pushing the table out of her way she is telling us how she has programmed her subconscious mind to reject the physical process of reproduction.

In this dream she is an au pair and the family to which she is assigned consists of a man and his daughter aged about eleven. Her period of service is coming to an end and there are only four weeks to go. 'Au pair' is a pun on the French 'Oh Pere' – father – so this dream is concerned with the effect her father had on her menstruation which began when she was eleven. 'Four weeks to go' suggests a monthly menstruation must go. This, and the reference to a low table, which also is a small column of figures, coupled with the swift passing of her time of service indicates her fertility is coming to an end.

The scene changes to the kitchen – digestion – and the man is mixing eggs in a large bowl – pun for bowel – and apparently making a cake – reproduction. The eggs are being mixed into a creamy mess. Mucous from the bowel merging with the dreamer's ovaries. He tells her they must leave the house to make way for visitors. She wonders where they are expected to go until he points to an extra kitchen detached from the main house. The window panes of the main kitchen were broken several times from the inside: a hysterectomy to which the dreamer's male aspect, the man in the dream, will eventually drive her.

Window panes broken inwards is a pun on 'bringing pain in on yourself' which the dreamer is doing by rejecting her femininity and all that goes with it.

This is typical of dreams where the dreamer judges herself with the harshness of the male aspect only. The mucous will eventually harden in the uterus and bring about the destruction of her reproduction system
(Key Words: Low, Rectangular, Four, Shove away.)

Generally speaking, dreams about female fertility involve the following:

* Bedroom, reference to mirrors, the assembly or production line at a factory, baggage clogging up the conveyor belt or carousel at an airport. (Influences from a former life are limiting the maternal instinct.)

* Reference to ovens, microwaves, and especially to damage of their working mechanism (uterus), photocopying machine.

* Reference to eggs, sometimes scrambled (ovaries) or a henhouse particularly if dirty with bird droppings (mucous from the colon getting into the system and limiting the production of eggs). Farm animals, rabbits with offspring, fertile fields, potted plants, seedlings, plant nurseries.

* People obviously looking at the dreamer as she attempts to do something creative or, conversely, people obviously ignoring her.

* A group of males (the dreamer's male aspect) squeezing her out in a situation involving seats. Female reproduction needs female hormones, which requires acceptance of the female aspect.

* A negative male (Father) leaving, ignoring, or turning his back on the dreamer. Apparent lack of acceptance by her father at birth can cause a woman to have a negative view of her own femininity/creativity.

* Various references to the digestive/elimination system, the colon in particular, showing the effects of mucous /toxins accumulating in the reproductive system.

* Front door (vagina), box or small room at the end of a hall (uterus)

* Dirty containers – cups, jugs, etc. – are symbolic of a negative view of femininity. The following examples are typical of this genre:

This dreamer is a woman in her thirties and both parents were disappointed with her gender at birth. The dream takes place in the gate lodge – pun for gynaecological – of the Phoenix Park, Dublin. This is a rich, fertile area, full of deer and other wildlife, a good symbol for the uterus and fertility generally. The gate lodge stands at the entrance of this enclosed park – representing the neck or entrance to the womb. In her dream the woman woke up to find that her boyfriend had left without saying good-bye. A sense of rejection – the boy friend plays the role of her father. She sees he had scrambled eggs before he left – the effect on her ovaries of her father's attitude .

(Key Words: *I am*: 'Scrambled' ; *I need*: 'Fertile'.)

This next dreamer works, in waking life, as a paediatric nurse with a number of babies in her care. In her dream she decides to take one of the babies home. As she takes it out to her car she realises there is nothing such as a cradle or baby seat, a receptacle for the child (ability to hold pregnancy) in the car (her body). There are a number of men around the car leaving her little room to manoeuvre (femininity pushed out). A queue of people (the colon) is entering the next door building. In the dream the other people are watching her closely as she tries to find space for the child.

Interpretation: This dreamer is, in a way, given a look inside her body. She is aware of the proximity of the colon (next door) to the uterus. Reference to it suggests it must be considered as a factor in her threatened infertility. (Cause and Effect) The people watching her recalls how critically she felt her femininity was regarded at birth.

Women who dream of ovens – especially if there is some difficulty with the functioning or mechanics – are most likely to develop problems with the uterus.

Pregnancy and giving birth is a great act of creativity. So, the preparation for making a cake, putting the mixture in the oven and finally, the emergence of the finished product is a symbolic parallel to the events of giving birth. Trouble with the uterus, as it appears in dreams, shows a link to a woman's attitude to her body and especially to her feminine creativity.

The all-important factor here is acceptance or otherwise of a woman's gender by her parents. If they are hoping for a boy and a girl arrives many parents cannot conceal a measure of disappointment. The new arrival picks this up and feels there must be something wrong with her body if her parents cannot accept it. It makes no difference if the parents accept her femininity later, the damage is done. A pattern of negative thinking is quickly established in the child in relation to her uterus, the symbol of that femininity, and is further linked to her desire (or lack of it) to create.

The influence of her father is of paramount importance to a baby girl. If he appears to reject her she may not accept herself and therefore limit her creativity throughout life. How he reacts to her earliest attempts at creativity is vital.

A woman who had a hysterectomy dreamt the following: She was sitting on a toilet bowl in the middle of the public street, feeling very uneasy, even though people passed by and took no notice of her. Later she was at home and two men called to take her microwave oven away. She wanted her money back on the guarantee because the oven was dirty. (Key word: Dirty)

Interpretation: The second part of the dream – her dissatisfaction with the microwave (dissatisfaction with her reproductive system) is easy to interpret but what about the toilet in the street? Dreams take us back to relive childhood experiences. To a child, having a bowl movement is a creative act. We can all remember the look of pride on a child's face when she produced 'an act of creativity' in the potty and then held it up to us for admiration and praise. When these early primitive attempts at creativity are ignored it reinforces the child's initial doubts about her capacity to create.

The mind has unlimited powers over the body and this negative thinking, coupled with the emotion it causes us to experience, has a detrimental effect on the body and, once again, we find the reference to elimination.

Negative thinking in relation to mothering can produce a similar effect in that it can be picked up from mother. Such is the case of a married woman with several children who had the following dream: She was on holiday in a boarding house with her children. Noticing that the door was hanging off the oven in the kitchen she called her children and accused them of causing the damage. Dreams taking place at holiday resorts usually want the dreamer to take a break or adapt a more relaxed attitude to her problems. The subject matter is mothering and how negative ideas cause problems. The idea referred to is along these lines: 'Why should I have to use my body as a boarding house for children' (pregnancy). This negative pattern of thought in relation to her body will eventually cause physical damage (the oven door).

I mentioned this latter case because it is an exception to the rule. Problems with the uterus are linked to self-acceptance and creativity – more often reflecting the influence of Dad. This dream illustrates instead some difficulty with mother. Where a mother gives (or neglects to give) of herself to her children it becomes an area of contention when mothering is the issue. If resentment is connected with mothering it tends to be reflected in the breast – as with cancer. A woman's reaction to her father in early life may have set her into a habitual mode of response which she now transfers to men in general. If she subconsciously holds the idea that men use, abuse, or even invade her body during sex and pregnancy, problems with her uterus may be expected ... but her dreams will warn her providing she pays attention.

STEPS TO HELP AVOID CANCER

Few would dispute that cancer is one of the greatest killers of our age. Dreams tell us when it threatens and go on to provide vital information on how we can stop the disease from developing – but we often overlook these warnings because we do not recognise them.

What causes cancer to start and why does the immune system fail to kill it? Repressed negativity is constantly creating minor outbreaks of the disease in our body which are swiftly quelled by the white blood cells and antibodies of our immune system. This happens so quickly and efficiently that the disease never comes to conscious awareness. Why then does the system break down and the cancer become terminal? The answer lies in our subconscious mind. Learning how to identify the minor outbreaks as they appear helps us to understand the disease and why it kills one person and not another.

The resentment, hurt, grief, or anger that eventually leads to cancer might be something that happened at birth or in early childhood. When looked at from the viewpoint of an adult this incident may seem trivial but because children cannot evaluate objectively what is happening when trauma occurs, such incidents tend to assume massive proportions. Counselling or hypnotic regression is helpful in getting this into perspective and, of course, dreams provide another viewpoint.

The causes of uncontrollable cancer may be seen as a five-phase development.

Phase One of the disease may begin by seemingly being ignored, critically judged, or apparently rejected, by our parent or parents at birth. This would be high on the list.

Unresolved grief at the death of our parents, anger or envy at their power over us, hurt or pain at apparent injustice within the family, sibling rivalry and other similar human emotions would seem unlikely candidates for causing cancer, but these are the very 'bones of contention' on which the budding disease thrives. It is only when dreams put such traumatic incidents into their proper place in the chain of Cause and Effect that we can appreciate their importance.

Phase Two is when we repress these feelings as being socially unacceptable or unworthy of us.

Phase Three occurs when the repressed negativity interferes with the clockwork mechanism of the body. Machinery designed to digest and eliminate food and other imports fails because we cannot mentally digest and eliminate.

The body is a physical reflection of the mind and if we are unable to assimilate new ideas and eliminate old ones then the physical process of assimilation and elimination comes under pressure. There are things about life we simply cannot 'stomach'. Hurt and pain we are unable to let go of and forgive cause harmless substances, normally taken into the body as nutrients, to turn into cancer-producing agents.

The body uses these pollutants to help create cancer and all that is left is to decide on what part of the body to attack. This is decided by the subconscious mind and the area designated will have some subconscious significance. The lungs might be chosen because we are tired of life, the genitals from sexual guilt, the breast if we have difficulty giving of ourselves, the stomach from an inability to accept, the colon because we cannot 'let go'. The list is lengthy.

Cancer appears as a lower animal or life form and the target area is shown in dreams as the location – the subconscious focus of attention, i.e. the part of the building into which the negative animal decides to eat. This area is accessed via the blood stream and pollution of the digestive/circulatory system appears as a factor.

A dirty or less than sterile environment is typical of cancer-warning dreams. Look for rats or worms eating dead bodies in filthy old houses (the body), weeds growing under neglected cement pathways (the colon).

Puns are also used to illustrate cancer in the target area. In one man's dream the action takes place on the deck of a naval destroyer – a pun indicating that the stomach/colon (navel) is the area at risk.

At other times the word 'cancer' is used directly in a dream as when a person in authority, usually a doctor or nurse, says you are at risk from the disease. This can only be taken literally if the dream goes on to elaborate how and why it is so. As every dream gives Cause and Effect it will not only indicate the possibility of contracting the disease but will also explain why you are at risk.

Phase Four is when the body decides either to accept the cancer and allow it to run its full course or to destroy it. Naturally this choice is made subconsciously since no rational mind would consciously accept cancer. Simply to dream of rats, or other negative life forms, and their growth or propagation, does not necessarily mean that a person is seriously at risk. It simply means that we need to resolve whatever is 'eating' us.

Other details from this, or similar dreams, makes it clear whether or not we subconsciously wish the cancer to survive. To kill, stun, or scare off the negative animal, pull the worm out of the body, or remove the weeds – taking care not to leave any roots in the ground – is a sign that we reject it. These are good symbols of a healthy immune system at work.

Does cancer still manage to survive? Only if we decide to let it. This is usually because we are tired of living or wish to make a statement by our death, to be a martyr. The latter option is more common with cancer in younger people and may appear in cancer-risk dreams. These include scenes of crucifixion, Jesus Christ, or someone making a statement in an extreme or extraordinary fashion.

The man who dreamt of the naval destroyer found himself climbing the mast and screaming protests at the people gathered on the deck beneath him.

In actual fact, being very ill at the time of his birth, he was thought to be dead and left to one side. His repressed anger at this apparent rejection lies at the base of his cancer risk. Subconsciously he is bringing it on himself as a statement to the world as his mind links being dead, or near dead, with getting attention.

Some personality types are more likely to get cancer than others. One tends to be extraordinarily tireless and self-sacrificing in pursuance of some worthy cause. These people will be found in crusades against injustice, anti-abortion rallies, and 'Save the Whale' marches or heroically walking for charity with, perhaps, one leg eaten off by cancer. Naturally they gain admiration and respect, but if we were to access their dreams we would find it is anger and resentment at apparent personal injustices in their youth that is actually 'eating' them rather than the cause in hand.

The second type of cancer-prone personality is the person who gives up on life. This occurs when incidents in the present simulate events from the past and reactivate old resentments, pain, and anger. When it all becomes too much to bear the sufferer 'pulls the plug' and develops a death wish.

Many of us are acquainted with stories of elderly couples in which one dies and, within a short period, the remaining partner gets cancer and follows. Is there an element of choice in this illness? Yes, but the option is taken subconsciously .

The self-defence mechanism responsible for fighting off disease is controlled by the subconscious. This part of the mind is super efficient and will continue to support the physical body unless it receives orders to the contrary. Outside factors can have such an emotional impact that the subconscious turns to a self-destruct mode. The death of a husband is upsetting for most women, but can be even more traumatic if it parallels the circumstances of their fathers' deaths. Particularly if the women did not, emotionally, fully resolve the original event.

Resentment at being passed over for a promotion in his job can cause a man to reactivate feelings of rejection by his parents. Infidelity in a marriage echoes injustice within the original family.

All or any of these feelings can produce a death wish and the subconscious, in true computer fashion, responds to this new impetus by retarding the immune system.

For most people dreams are the only way of knowing what is going on in this area of the mind. A death wish appears in dreams as puns, locations, colours or characters. Indeed everything in a cancer-warning dream must be examined for indications of this anti-life bias.

A woman of my acquaintance was in a pre-cancer state with benign lumps forming on her breasts. She dreamt that she was pregnant and walking along Kill Lane, a Dublin suburb. I recall similar dreams taking place in a slaughterhouse (self-destruction) and cemetery (giving up on the self).

Cancer sometimes appears in dreams as an unpleasant shade of purple i.e. red / black mix – a strange alignment of life (red) and death (black).

Characters also indicate how we feel about life. One of Sigmund Freud's patients, named Anna, dreamt she was being attacked by the goddess Diana (die Anna). Dreaming about people known to us who died from the disease could further underline this life/ death dichotomy.

To understand cancer we need to appreciate the emotional intensity that children experience at birth and shortly thereafter. An infant who feels threatened is unable to rationalise without reference to similar emotions experienced in former lives. The newborn searches for a parallel situation in the long term memory banks of the subconscious mind and emotions appropriate to a life and death situation are brought forward in time and applied to apparently trivial incidents.

Having the umbilical cord tighten around the neck is frightening, enough but it would be even more so if we were hanged to death in a former life.

Not being acceptable because of having a female body is frustrating, but we would feel this even more intensely if, in a former life, such an attitude resulted in someone's death. If a child feels he has no control over his life he is able to programme his subconscious to self-destruct in a given set of circumstances. This is not unlike a death sentence on hold – or suspended pending further investigation of what life has to offer. If it becomes too much to bear, if he cannot control his world or the people in it, the option to activate the death programme can be taken up. It is rather like a built-in escape clause. At any time such events as the death of a loved one, financial setbacks, marital breakdown, career problems, or any other experience which the person feels deeply about may be sufficient to push the button and begin the countdown to death.

Cancer can even be used as a weapon, to make a point, be a martyr, to punish parents or others for real or imagined wrongdoing. The excuses to feel resentment are virtually endless.

It may seem strange that a child just starting out in life would consider death in this way but it should be remembered that the newcomer came from a better place and carries the memory of how pleasant it was on the spirit plane. Life on Earth may not seem as precious at a young age as it will as an adult. The infant may choose to opt out and become another cot death or to simply implant the death wish in his or her subconscious. In later life this programming may be forgotten by the conscious mind but the subconscious is still programmed and will, like a time bomb, await further lethal orders. In the meantime whatever 'eats' or annoys this individual will continue to produce minor outbreaks of cancer which never come to maturity.

Hypnosis is a useful tool in understanding the nature of cancer. A woman who dreamt of a squirrel eating into her leg came to me for hypnotic regression. We discovered she was a Franciscan priest in a former life and that her present mother had been a powerful politically-minded cleric who controlled her life.

She carried great anger and resentment at the level of control used against her. Is it any wonder when she met her mother in this life, subconsciously recognising her as an old rival, she felt such frustration and resentment at her own powerlessness?

This woman's dreams contained no death wish so the health warning was not urgent but it took time and effort on her part to resolve her feelings about her mother. Had she not done so the danger would have remained because cancer-prone people are capable of producing a death wish even in old age as they get tired of life. They allow what is 'eating' them to finish the job.

Phase Five of the cancer development risk may be applied to all illness but is especially applicable to this disease. It is 'The Learning Process' and involves self-examination and a review of one's personal philosophy.

Important lessons are inevitably learned even if they remain in the subconscious and never come to conscious awareness. Why me? How can God allow innocent people to suffer such pain? What did I do to deserve this? These are frequently asked questions, but it is only when the patient realises he is responsible for his own suffering that he can begin the healing process. If extreme reactions to his parent's shortcomings brought on the illness perhaps he could be more moderate, more forgiving, more tolerant, more patient.

These lessons are illustrated in dreams and we must look for Healing Agents displaying the necessary good qualities. Colours like beige, blue, pink and yellow further emphasise the need to reconsider our position in relation to tolerance, philosophy, love and letting go.

In Summary: Look for the following four telltale signs to locate the cancer risk as it appears in dreams.

Repressed Negativity: This is anger, hurt, guilt, grief or resentment, usually linked to a parent. The negative feeling is unexpressed and locked away in the subconscious.

Watch for something obnoxious in closets, cupboards, underground, in bottles or other containers, especially if the colour black appears. As some of this negativity may have roots in previous incarnations we can expect to find characters dressed in period costumes, old-fashioned furniture, buildings, etc.

Digestive/Circulatory Pollution: A toxic or slow-moving colon can provide an ideal breeding ground for cancer which is then transported around the body, through the bloodstream, to a symbolically significant destination. This process can appear in a dream as a vehicle carrying negative life forms from an underground sewer to a specified location on a map via a network of 'arterial' roads. In such dreams the map represents the dreamer's body. The mouth of a river in the upper half could represent the throat while an estuary in the lower half may represent the uterus – particularly if ships are 'berthed' there. A specified destination on this map indicates the area of the body which is most at risk from this disease.

Negative life or growth forms: These are shown as mice, rats, squirrels, worms, weeds – even seditious propaganda – usually the growth of a lower life form or negative animal although they can also appear as human.

A policeman who was undergoing therapy dreamt that two criminals (cancer) had been arrested (the development of the disease had been temporality halted or 'arrested' – pun). But when it came to the interrogation (getting at the truth), charging and processing of the guilty parties, he was very lax in his duty. His own sense of guilt is partly responsible for this cancer-prone situation. Generally speaking, dealing in some way with the negative life form is a hopeful sign in these dreams.

List negative life or growth forms as 'Key Words'. To identify areas at risk look for what these organisms are linked to, or associated with, in the dream.

The Death Wish: If combined with the previous symbols this increases the risk. It can take many forms but, in essence, represents a perverse attitude to life such as following a dead relative or spouse up a flight of stairs. Or carrion crows burrowing into the chest area and a reluctance by the dreamer or others to pull them out. The sufferer may find himself unnecessarily putting his life in danger, courting death, or showing a disregard to preserving his life. Remember to look for puns.

SAMPLE DREAMS

Here is your opportunity to put Secret Language of the Soul into practise by applying what you have learned to the following sample dreams. For your convenience my interpretation of each is listed in the next chapter but do work out your own before checking. Doing this exercise will help you to find out how well you understand the process. Please do not be disheartened if it seems difficult at first. I may have many years experience and you are beginning – but I did not have this book to help me!

1.   A businessman in his early Fifties, whose family had a history of heart weakness, dreamt the following: He was in a shop conducting business with another man who was putting him under pressure. As they spoke a loud noise rang out from the back of the building and suddenly a woman passed by. He went to the back to investigate and found that a pipe had burst in the central heating system.

Later he found himself in an open green field, carrying a child on his back, and knew he had to climb over a wall to get where he was going. He also had the distinct impression that he had already done this on a number of previous occasions. However, this time the wall seemed that little bit higher, the child that little bit heavier, and he only just managed to get over the wall. He realised he wasn't as fit as he used to be.

2.   A woman dreamt she was walking in the vicinity of Trinity College – a 16th century University in Dublin. Some workmen were digging in the grounds and unearthing fabulous treasure.

3.   A man in his forties often saw spirit forms at the end of his bed at night. They never spoke or made a sound and this terrified him. One night he dreamt a beautiful woman came into the room, plugged in a T.V. set, and turned up the sound. He described her as having 'huge, saucer-shaped ears' and she also mentioned his own ears.

4.   A man dreamed he was in a hayshed that was also a cafe. He thought the service was rather slow – he had to wait an hour and a half to be fed. A stack of damp hay stood to one side of the room and he noticed that he was sitting on a pile of peat that was covered in mould. The floor of the hayshed was also covered with this mould.

5. In one woman's dream she returns to the family home. She is surprised to find that the walls and floor were covered in a dull brown or faecal coloured wallpaper and carpet. The floor area is completely covered with swamp grass and soggy, water-logged soil. She went into the kitchen where the old window, facing out the back has been replaced with a narrower aperture and here too, the floor is covered with swamp grass.

   As she looked out the window, she noticed a team of female soccer players exercising. The dreamer then went into a narrow passage to the side of the house and, in doing so, partially blocked the movement of a car trying to come out. She 'knew' the occupants were in great danger.

6.   It is encouraging to see signs of improvement in dreams, as the dreamer undergoes treatment. A man who suffered from a dangerously unhealthy circulation system found that sauna, dietary changes and exercise improved his condition. After realising the problem and deciding to heal his elimination system, he had the following dream: He was going out for a meal. A car was jacked-up by the side of the road and he was approached by the female driver who asked him to help change the wheel. She had emptied the contents of a tool box onto the roadway; as well as tools, there were a huge number of rusty nuts, screws and nails.

The dreamer searched through the tools to find the correct spanner to loosen the wheel nuts and get the car going again. He was successful.

7.   Many men and women have reported the following dream: I was trying to do an exam at school and getting in a panic because I was not fully prepared / had not done enough study / was running out of time.

8.   A young wife, with one child from a traumatic pregnancy, was terrified of becoming pregnant again. She dreamt she was on stage with a famous hypnotist. A heavy boulder had been placed on her stomach and she was expected to bear the weight of it. The hypnotist told her she could take it. She was afraid and ran from the theatre. When she reached home she found the front of the house in darkness but the sun was shining brightly in the back garden. Everything looked different. A neighbour was putting out his empty milk bottle and, although she felt she should know him, she did not. Nor did he recognise her.

9.   A man who recently discovered he had the gift of healing, the 'laying on of hands', dreamt he was balanced

precariously on top of a huge gasometer. Although a 'beautiful golden sun' was shining the dreamer had no time to admire it as he tried to maintain his footing. His former employer – 'a nasty old lady' shared this perch with him and insisted he 'get down'.

10. A woman dreamt she was sitting alone in a moonlit open-air restaurant. Couples sit at small candle-lit tables covered with green tablecloths. The area is surrounded by a strange conglomeration of irregular-shaped buildings with a 'motley collection of inhabitants'. Like the buildings, the people mix well despite their obvious differences. A radio is playing. The guest of honour arrives. He is a prominent barrister. He approaches the dreamer's table and introduces his wife to her.

11. A woman who was practising 'hands on' healing had a dream in which she was crouched 'in the foetal position' in the hallway of the house where she was born. She was waiting for a delivery. Eventually the postman arrived and left an envelope. When she opened it she found a letter and her deceased father's gold watch.

12. A man had the following dream. 'I was walking up a flight of stairs. John, my work mate, who I would describe as a weak sort of person, was with me. I realised that I was in danger because some of the steps were missing'.

13. In this dream a businessman was in a neglected, dilapidated church. He immediately thought he could make a profit if he bought the floorboards and the fittings for scrap. He approached someone he found there with an offer. The person simply pointed upstairs. As the dreamer climbed the stairs he was confronted by a bishop who

directed him to a sale of work (handicrafts). These items were laid out on large tables for display. The dreamer's attention was drawn to a beautiful painting in shades of blue, purple and indigo.

14. A woman had a dream in which a rat was gnawing into the front door of a very dingy, grubby house.

15. A bachelor with somewhat untidy habits had the following dream: He was in his kitchen and opened the fridge door. In his waking life the inside of this man's fridge is usually in a dirty condition with bits and blobs of milk and cream staining the floor and walls. It was likewise in his dream but as he opened the door he noticed two mice inside. They were both green. One mouse, startled by the intrusion, ran off. The other was dead and he noticed that it was a mutant in that it appeared to be a cross between a mouse and a rasher. Extending down its back, as part of its anatomy, was a mane made out of the fatty rind of bacon.

16. Here the dreamer is a woman in her forties who, although interested in politics was in fact restricted to housework. She dreamt that she was at a ceremony to mark the launch of a new book written by a prominent female politician. A crowd had gathered and there was a gala atmosphere. The place was decorated with green bunting.

The dreamer then noticed that she was wearing an apron which was covered with pimples as if it had a rash. As she looked down at it she noticed a 'dirty looking squirrel' eating its way into her leg. She was horrified to see that it had burrowed itself right into the flesh. She woke up at this point.

17. A pretty, 24 year old investigative journalist had a dream in which she was a man working in an underground coalmine in what she described as a 'grey metropolis'. She loaded bags of coal onto a lorry for distribution throughout the country. The bags were tied but she knew they also contained secret revolutionary material and propaganda. She was a spy working against the country in which she lived. Then the scene changed and she found herself in a hotel room. She had written a book and a group of journalists were there to interview her about it but she had no time to talk to them. She was packing her bags and leaving on the next train even though she knew it was destined for Belsen concentration/extermination camp.

18. This dreamer is a woman in her late forties. Her husband John had died two years prior to the dream. It begins in the living room. The dreamer is sitting in her usual chair when she notices John trying to open the door as if to leave the room. When he succeeds in doing so she decides to follow him and make him something to eat. In the kitchen she gets a shock. The frying pan has fallen off the cooker onto the floor. When she picks it up she notices the family crest on the inside of the pan. (In reality the woman had no idea what her particular family crest looked like.) She sees that the pan is corroded and eaten away with rust in the area of the crest.

19. A 28-year-old man who had been adopted as a baby dreamt he was talking to a man of around his own age. As the man spoke the dreamer noticed an aperture in the side of the other's neck with what looked like the tail of a worm making its way inward. He noticed the man's eyeballs turn 'milk white' as this happened. Otherwise the man seemed oblivious to the worm. The dreamer determined to try to

help him. Some little time later the head of the worm appeared on the other side of the man's neck. The dreamer grabbed the head and, with great effort, pulled out the creature. It fell to the ground and began to grow larger and larger. Some men chased it and beat it with sticks. As they did it took the form of an ugly old woman.

20 (A). A woman recounted this dream : 'I was staying in lodgings in war-torn Berlin. There was a tense atmosphere everywhere with unexploded bombs and mines all over the place. My landlady was an enemy agent and had the place booby-trapped. I was opening a can of food with great apprehension expecting it to explode at any moment'.

20 (B). From a woman in her mid thirties: 'I met a man at a disco, invited him home for coffee, and was irritated to find my mother there waiting for me. She began to ask my guest awkward questions about his eligibility for marriage. Did he have a house? What was he earning? I became very annoyed with her. The kitchen was old-fashioned with a Fifties-style cooker and fridge. Milk was boiling over on the stove and falling onto the floor. I opened the door of the fridge to find a bowl of lumpy white slime.'

21. One woman dreamt she was in her garden drinking tea when bird droppings fell into it polluting the contents.

22. A 12 year old boy recounted this dream: 'I was looking at my mother washing the dishes. She took a cheese grater in her mouth and sucked it. It was flat on one side and curved on the other. I knew it would poison her.

23. A woman dreamt she was in her bedroom. It was the same as in reality except that it contained a male urinal. She was furiously scrubbing this with a harsh abrasive cleaner to such an extent that the enamel coating was wearing off.

24. A woman who came to me for treatment had the following dream. She was buying a new house and, as the dream opens, was viewing the property. Inside the front door was a room with two fireplaces – two hearths. A lovely pink rug lay on the floor. A very positive lady then showed her around and presented her with a picture of the Sacred Heart. The woman then showed our dreamer a picture of a naked female fully immersed in water.

25. 'I found myself having my fortune told in what appeared to be a native American tepee although it looked more like an Egyptian pyramid from the inside. I didn't think much of the 'reading' or the uninspiring appearance of the woman fortune-teller who wore a black costume. However, when I got outside, my attention was drawn to a beautiful eagle that was soaring majestically in the sky and looking down from an incredible height.'

The Interpretations follow, with corresponding numbers, in Chapter Sixteen.

THE INTERPRETATIONS

1. The shop building represents the physical body of the
dreamer. A central heating system consisting of a series of
pipes circulating throughout the building is a good symbol
for the circulatory system. The dream is a warning of future
problems with the heart if action is not taken in the present
to eliminate the cause – which can also be found. There is a
sense of urgency and pressure and the fact that it takes place
in a shop or business premises with another man suggests
the dreamer's father put him other pressure to succeed in
business. Negative male and female characters indicate the
effect of parents on the dreamer.

The sudden noise from the back of the building indicates
a shock from the past. In this case it was the death of his
mother (the woman passing) which was largely responsible
for his condition. Pressure to succeed from his father and
the trauma of his mother's death in his early youth set the
pattern for future heart trouble

Notice how, in this dream, all the symbols are linked to
show Cause and Effect. There is no logical connection
between the shop premises, the man doing business, the
woman passing and the burst central heating pipes. Yet it is
a rule of dream interpretation that all symbols are linked
into a chain, which invariably shows the cause of the
dreamer's problems. This is the case with the wall which is
his defensive barrier and was set up at the age of the child
he carries.

2. The subject matter indicated by the location of this dream – a university – is the dreamer's higher knowledge and wisdom gained in former lives (the ancient building) that now lays buried in the long-term memory of her subconscious mind.

She is being guided to 'unearth' this very precious information by meditation.

3. The television refers to the dreamer's gift of clairvoyance – the ability to 'see' beyond the range of most people. The Guide/Healing Agent wants him to adapt a more 'female' (receptive) approach to his gift, to 'tune in' (plugging in the T.V.) and listen to the sound.

After having this dream the man took the offered advice and learned to listen to the spirits who wanted to use him as a channel. In doing so one of his ears, which had been deaf for twenty years, was cured.

4. The hayshed/cafe represents the dreamer's digestion. Slow service indicates a slow-moving bowel. The stack of damp hay points to a backlog in the digestive tract and the mould suggests fungus – Candida Albicans.

The dictionary defines mould as a growth caused by dampness and this is indeed a fair description of Candida. It is a condition which grows out of faecal matter left in a stagnant state in the body for years as indicated by the stack of hay in the dream. Similarly, the psychosomatic cause of the condition is mental stagnation or a reluctance to move on to new ideas.

5. The dreamer returning to her family home indicates a reluctance to let go of the past. This frequently precedes elimination difficulties. The colour of the wallpaper and carpet points to poor elimination.

The state of grass in a dream reflects the state of the dreamer's blood stream. Lumpy, clumpy grass would indicate poor circulation, and the colour green tries to heal the circulatory system. Here our attention is drawn to swampy or undrained soil and grass, so the subject matter is the state of the lymph glands. The kitchen denotes her digestion and the narrow window looking out onto the back garden indicates a limited and retrogressive outlook on life.

Holding onto the past and an unwillingness to look to the future in a positive way, lies at the bottom of this dreamer's problem. The footballers are healing agents, highlighting the need to exercise to improve her circulation and elimination. References to sport or exercise, cycling, exercise shoes or clothing, is typical of these types of dreams and the ability to forgive, release or let go, is part of the female aspect of all humans, regardless of gender, hence the football players were women.

Finally, her 'knowing' that the car's occupants were 'in great danger' indicates she is subconsciously warned of the danger of blood clotting. Since everything is linked in a dream it is possible to see the problems created by lymphatic clogging.

6. Going out for a meal addresses the dreamer's digestion. The rusty nuts, screws and nails indicate digestive rubbish. In finding the spanner his dream reassured him that he had found the right tool (his new lifestyle). The wheel nuts represent his lymph glands. Loosening the nuts on a central heating radiator would have the same meaning and it would be a positive sign even if water were released from the circulating pipes. He got the car (his body) going again.

7. A very common dream where the dreamer is being told by his or her Higher Self that there is a lack of diligence in

getting on with one's spiritual life purpose. We have failed to adequately prepare for the adventure of life. Watch for Guides in this or subsequent dreams. Their example, word, gesture, requirements of the exam and / or interviewers, indicates what we are meant to learn in life.

8. This young mother's being anxious on stage, rather than in the audience, suggests performance anxiety. The heavy rock she is supposed to hold on her stomach represents the burden of responsibility for being an adult as in childbearing, etc.

The hypnotist, a person of great confidence, is her Healing Agent who reassures her. He is also her Guide and indicates by his profession that she also has this gift.

Her flight from the theatre (and the responsibility of adult life) is causing her to lose her grip on reality. This is shown as the once-familiar neighbour becoming a stranger. The darkness at the front of the house suggests negativity (fear) in relation to facing life. The back of the house is sunlit. This dreamer subconsciously longs to return to the carefree days of childhood.

She admitted to having suffered three nervous breakdowns to date. Her dream indicates she is heading for a fourth. A person who is capable of hypnotising generally has a powerful mind and imagination which, if undisciplined, can lead to trouble.

9. A gasometer that provides power for a large number of people is a good symbol of the dreamer's spiritual gift or power which is to heal others. This is emphasised by the 'golden sun' – another symbol of healing and power. The dreamer is uneasy with this power (unsure of his footing). His former female employer (mother), playing the role of his shadow self, tries to bring him down.

In waking life his mother's disempowering influence continues to limit his potential.

10. The dreamer is a therapeutic counsellor in waking life and this is indicated by the profession of her Guide in the dream. A barrister is often referred to as 'counsel'. This gift is also indicated by the colour green and the merging of incongruous buildings and people – an ability to harmonise conflict within people which helps the dreamer in her counselling work. However, this dream indicates that she approaches her job from an intellectual (male aspect) angle and is now being encouraged to accept the female approach – indicated by the barrister's wife. The moon and candlelight refer to her natural intuition while the radio indicates clairaudience. Through using her gift this dreamer will learn to 'open herself' emotionally (the open-air restaurant) to others.

11. This is a rebirthing dream as can be seen from the foetal position in the hallway (birth canal). The dream is telling this woman she was born to be a healer and the profession of her Guide – a postman – indicates she is also a channel or spirit medium. The letter is a message from her dead father saying it is time (his gold watch) to open up her ability (the envelope) and extend her horizons. The dreamer's stance and situation – in the box-shaped hallway – suggest she is limiting herself.

12. This is typical of someone with back problems. In this dream the stairs represent the dreamer's backbone which appears to be somewhat defective – the missing steps. John symbolises the negative effect of Dad in not supporting the dreamer in childhood and, since all the symbols are linked, this lack of support led to his back problems.

13. The decrepit state of the church reflects neglect of the dreamer's spirituality and life purpose. His philosophy has become too materialistic – selling the floorboards. These represent his understanding – under where he stands. He is asked to raise his consciousness (going upstairs).

The Guide appearing as a bishop, and use of the colour purple in the painting, indicates the dreamer's leadership qualities. He was born to be an entrepreneur, to provide employment (the sale of work) for others and, in the process, expected to learn to share himself with others (the large tables).

The colour indigo indicates his psychic ability. Strangely enough, this colour often appears in the dreams of successful businessmen who frequently use this 'knack' to help them predict the outcome of business ventures. They are completely unaware that this 'hunch' is, in fact, a spiritual gift.

Finally, the colour blue (in the painting) refers to the dreamer's philosophy of life which, in this case, needs improving.

14. This dream indicates sexual guilt or frigidity in the dreamer. Negative symbols are the rat (lower life form), dingy, grubby house (attitude to her body). To a female 'the front door' represents the vagina. This dreamer's mental/emotional attitude to sex would put her at risk from cancer of the cervix.

If health problems are genetic reference is sometimes made to jeans – pun on genes – so if someone was wearing black (negative) jeans in the setting described in the above dream it would be fair to assume that the problem was inherited.

15. This dream is very important for a number of reasons. The dirty inside of the dream fridge indicates digestive rubbish. Then it shows the connection between cancer (the mutated mouse) and animal fat (the rasher). The aberrated form of the animal identifies it as a renegade cancer cell. The colour green shows the incompatibility (inability to share) of the fat/cancer cell to the body. Generally speaking if you are taking foods or drink which do not agree with you they will sometimes appear as green. Cancer will often be seen as something eating away inside you, symbolically suggesting negative emotion such as resentment eating into or corroding your sense of well being. This often takes place within a confined space indicating that the negativity is repressed or not brought out into the open. The repression aspect is shown here as activity within a fridge and the healing activity of the dream is, of course opening the door. Another way this may be illustrated in dreams would be a reference to a press (pun for repressed), packed suitcases, bottles (a pun for bottled-up) and so on.

The healing activities in dreams of this kind i.e. opening doors (bringing subconscious negativity to conscious awareness), rising in the air above a situation (getting an objective view), taking photographs or writing a book (re-evaluating or reviewing) are literally saving your life in that they encourage your subconscious to destroy the cancers.

In the dream we can see how opening the door of the fridge frightened off one green mouse and killed the other – Rule Two. This is typical of many cancer-warning dreams. They ask you to bring out into the open whatever is 'eating you' in the way of resentment and having done so take a look at it, re-evaluate it and let it go. This 'letting go' will also speed up the physical process of elimination.

16. The author, a prominent politician, is the dreamer's mother. The book created by the politician is herself. Since everything reflects the dreamer, this does not concern itself with the mother but with herself and her reaction to this parent. The dream, as many do, takes the dreamer back to her birth (the launch of the new book). It also recreates the atmosphere (the gala event) of that day. Green bunting suggests jealousy (green -eyed monster). The dreamer, at the time of her birth, was jealous of mother's power (politicians being people of power) and this craving for power stayed with her into adult life. Now, when she is confined to housework and looking after her children, she gets irritated. An apron covered with red pimples is an interesting symbol. On one hand it suggests mother, mothering and housework, but on another level it indicates circulatory pollution. The squirrel, of course speaks for itself and the implied health warning – of cancer – must be clear enough at this stage.

17. We can see several symbols of concentrated negativity – the bags of coal, packed suitcases and concentration camp (a pun). Coal itself is a concentrated form of energy to be released as fire, therefore it is is a symbol for unexpressed emotion. But coal is black so the energy would be negative. To further emphasise the repression aspect she tells us that the coal is packed into bags which are then tied.

The grey metropolis being the capital (head) means she functions mainly in her mind and represses her emotions – grey is the symbol of denial of emotion.

In distributing sedition throughout the country she is sewing the seeds for future trouble to spread throughout her body. Propaganda spreads and multiplies and can destroy the order and Government of a country. Therefore it can be seen to strongly symbolise the cancer which she is putting into her blood stream (the road network). Once again we find circulatory pollution.

This work being done underground (a pun on undermining) and working for an underground organisation (another pun), tells us that the danger is in her subconscious and below the level of her everyday awareness. In other words she doesn't consciously know what she is doing to herself.

That she has her bags packed for Belsen hardly needs interpretation. This is the death wish. Her mental /emotional state is taking her to her own destruction. She is going to be the sacrificial lamb and since the train represents her digestive/elimination stream we can see that the cancer has already picked out its destination. This death train represents the target area – the colon. The other journalists are Healing Agents who would be expected to carry the quality of objectivity which she needs to exercise in relation to herself. The idea of writing a book is another device to encourage her to engage in research – to review or re-evaluate her situation before she destroys herself. Why is she doing this? In the dream she is male, therefore anger at her femininity is the bottom line – the old story of parents being disappointed at the gender of their offspring.

NOTE: This dreamer came to me for hypnosis and regression back to her birth confirmed her frustration at being female. Further regression back to a former life was even more illuminating. In 19th century Britain she was also female and lived in a farming community where she was greatly distressed by what she felt was the unjust way landlords treated their tenants. She tried to organise a revolt. Being female her advice was unheeded. The peasantry took action but without proper leadership the uprising was quickly suppressed.

In one session she tearfully recalled the public hanging of a tenant protester.

Anger and frustration lay at the core of this dreamer's cancer risk. Happily, once this came out into the open her attitude changed. She now fully accepts her femininity and has released herself of negative feelings from the past. The pattern of her dreams has also changed for the better and shows that the danger from cancer has receded.

18. Two weeks after having had this dream the woman was diagnosed as having cancer of the pancreas

The exact words used by the dreamer are very important because they contain the puns which very often reveal the essence of the dream. The most obvious pun in this one is 'pan crest' – for pancreas. The cancer appears as the rust which has eaten into and corroded the 'pan crest'.

The fact this takes place in the kitchen indicates the digestive system as the most likely place for the cancer to take hold and the pancreas is part of that system.

The death wish is implied in her account of leaving the living room to follow her dead husband. The shock of the pan falling to the ground symbolises the shock of her husband's death linking with the memory of her father and whatever unresolved grief or emotion lay buried there.

As you will see from cancer dreams the death wish is often contained in the location of the dream which, it is worth remembering indicates the subject matter – living or dying in this case – and the dreamer's state of mind. Also, please keep in mind Rules Two and Three – that everything in the dream is linked to show cause and effect and that the dreamer is responsible for what happens – in this case the cancer. It may seem callous to 'blame' the sufferer for his own cancer but it is true that we create our own illnesses and by accepting that we can begin the process of creating our own cures.

19. This man was holding a deep rooted but unexpressed resentment at his mother for having rejected him.

Milk in any dream refers to mother while the colour white symbolises perfection. The negative old lady shows how his perfectionist or 'should be' attitude to his adoption is 'eating away' inside him. There is not, however, a death wish in the dream and until something else happens, like the death of a spouse or some other shock, he will continue to fight off minor outbreaks of cancer. In his case the most vulnerable area is the throat which holds the voice box and represents expression.

An important issue must be addressed here. If you have a cancer-type risk how urgent is the health warning? How high is the risk of cancer?

Please remember that dreams are warnings and attempts at self healing and, as far as predicting the future is concerned, are not cast iron certainties. The main purpose of dreams is to allow us deviate from a mental/emotional line which may lead to illness.

Thinking about your dream, interpreting it correctly, meditating on it, following the advice and guidance contained in it, could be sufficient to bring about such a deviation in which case the dream will not come true. You may not become ill. Further dreams will confirm or refute this. If no mention is made of dealing with or destroying the negative life form there is still no need to worry. You may be killing off cancers without this actually appearing in your dreams.

There is a greater urgency or a higher risk if the cancer-type dreams include a death wish. Such dreams should be taken more seriously, but there is still no need to panic. Dreams will indicate health risks many years in advance of the actual onset of the illness so there is usually plenty of time to take remedial action. However, if we wilfully refuse to forgive those who hurt us and stubbornly insist on holding onto our grievances the dreams will become dramatic – even nightmarish. The frequency of such dreams is a fair indication of the urgency of the health warning.

20 (A & B). In light of what we know about the connection between birth, mother's and our own emotional state at the time of the first feed, and the creation of mucous, is it any wonder 'Dreamer A' had a dozen different food allergies?

In both dreams we can detect a negative atmosphere in the home circumstances – shown as war-time Berlin in Dream A and the old-style kitchen in Dream B. The first dreamer's reaction to mother (the landlady being mother in disguise) was one of fear and mistrust while the second dreamer responded to her mother with irritation.

Both reactions, however were linked to food – the can about to explode in the first dream and the boiling milk in the second. In Dream B we see how irritation with mother made her milk boil and turn into mucous – the lumpy slime in the fridge. The fridge, a solid object used for containing food, is a good symbol for the stomach. This is an allergy to milk/dairy produce caused by the dreamer's reaction to her mother. In Dream A we see how the fearful atmosphere in the home caused by mother is 'exploding' the food in the dreamer's body.

In dreams where food items explode or turn into poison it is reasonable to look for food allergies. Dreams, through highlighting cause and effect show allergies to be caused by our reaction to parents. This is not unreasonable when you consider that we receive our first meal from mother who in the process unconsciously passes onto us her own fears and anxieties.

21. Generally speaking, if we are taking food or drink to which we are (even unconsciously) allergic we can expect to find something unpleasant happening to it in dreams. In reality this dreamer admits to drinking too much tea. It is not unusual, in dreams, for unpleasant fluids to drop from the ceiling onto cream cakes, white bread, or whatever food or drink you are being instructed to avoid for the sake of your health.

22. This dreamer is a young asthmatic who has an allergic reaction to cheese.

Seeing his mother being poisoned by the cheese grater indicates his allergic reaction not just to cheese but also to his mother. The cheese grater being flat one side and semi-cylindrical on the other represents the lungs or the chest area of the dreamer's body. In asthmatics the body feels threatened by invasion from outside agents such as dust, smoke and other pollution. It forms a defensive wall in the sinuses and lungs to keep this invader out. Milk, cheese and dairy products are turned into mucous which is used to make this defensive barrier. Unfortunately this defense measure also inhibits breathing.

23. The bedroom represents her sexuality and also her reproductive system. The urinal, as a solid object, represents her uterus. What she was trying to do, in aggressively cleaning it, was to rid herself of a sense of being used and abused. In the process she was damaging the enamel coating – the lining of her uterus. Subconsciously she regarded herself and her femininity as something a man might use with his penis – as he used the urinal.

This dreamer has trouble accepting her femininity and sexuality. Three weeks after having that dream she suffered a miscarriage.

24. This is a healing dream asking the woman to open (expose) her heart like Jesus. This literally gives her the courage to open up emotionally. The beautiful house she is asked to accept with its two hearths (hearts –a play on words) represents an enhanced ability to radiate warmth (emotion) and love (the pink rug). Female characters indicate the dreamer's emotions while males show the dreamer's state of mind. The naked female here symbolises exposed emotion and her total immersion in water symbolises the total commitment to life needed by this dreamer.

25. The dreamer has the gifts of prophesy and clairvoyance.

She has the ability to 'see' the past, present and future as indicated by the great visual range of the soaring eagle (guiding ideal). She has used these in at least two previous incarnations – as a native American and Egyptian. However, this time she is expressing her distrust of the gifts by her negative description of the fortune-teller (her Guide). The structure of the tepee/pyramid suggests the need to achieve oneness or to focus the mind – as the wide base tapers to a point at the top (guiding ideal).

You now have direct access to the basics of Secret Language of the Soul, humankind's oldest form of communication. Use it wisely and well to help yourself and others.

FURTHER READING

Cutting the Ties that Bind Workbook, by Phyllis Krystal.
1995. Samuel Weiser Inc. York Beach, Maine, USA.

The Grand Design, Part 1, by Patrick Francis.
1987. Regency Press, 125, High Holborn, London.

Dreams Your Magic Mirror, by Elisie Sechrist.
1968. Warner Books, New York.

The various books and publications on Edgar Cayce
issued by the Association for Research and
Enlightenment, Virginia Beach, USA.

DREAMS – SECRET LANGUAGE OF THE SOUL

Dream Interpretation Newsletter

The focus of our monthly Dream Interpretation Newsletter is to keep you prac-
ticed in interpreting your dreams. We invite dreams from readers and in each
issue explain techniques for their interpretation and give advice on how to follow their instructions. We also explore different dimensions of dreams and
expand on areas covered in the book and more.

With your first issue you also receive a free bonus issue. We feel so sure that
you will enjoy your subscription that we make the following guarantee: If you
cancel your subscription after receiving the first issue and before receiving the
second we will refund you the unused portion of your subscription.

PC Programme

Our PC Programme, which is available from January 1997, allows you record
your dreams while keeping them safe from prying eyes. It comes with the
Aisling Interpretation Engine which uses a database of symbols to give you
hints on the meaning of your dreams. 30% of profits from the sale of this pro-
gram will be donated to Famine Relief in Africa.

Audio Tapes

A number of meditation tapes by the author will be available from January
1997. Side 1 of each contains an explanation and introduction. Side 2 consists
of deep meditation and/or regression. All these tapes are designed to enhance
your life and awareness. 50% of profits from the sale of these tapes will be
donated to Famine Relief in Africa.

Order Form – Valid Until 31 December 1997

Tick the appropriate box(es) and fill in your name and address below.

☐ Tape 1: *Re-empowering the Self* (Regression to Birth & Early Childhood) £9
☐ Tape 2: *Eliminating Negative Former Life Influences*
          (Regression to Former Life) £9
☐ Tape 3: *Gifts, Talents and Healing from Former Lives*
          (Regression to Positive Former Life) £9
☐ Tape 4: *Communicating with Spirit Guides* £9
☐ 1 year Newsletter subscription (13 issues) £10
☐ 6 month Newsletter Subscription (7 issues) £18
☐ Book (add. copies): *Dreams – Secret Language of the Soul* (inc. P&P) £9
☐ PC Dream Interpretation Programme £20
☐ Please send me a current order form and details of courses and
    workshops in my area (no charge)

Name: _____	Please post this form along with your postal order/cheque to:
Address: _____	
_____	*Aisling Dream Interpretation*
Tel.: _____	PO Box 5373 Dublin 24